LOCKED HOMES
EMPTY SCHOOLS

THE IMPACT OF DISTRESS SEASONAL MIGRATION
ON THE RURAL POOR

SMITA
PHOTOGRAPHS: PRASHANT PANJIAR
FOREWORD: AMARTYA SEN

zubaan

Locked Homes, Empty Schools
The Impact of Distress Seasonal Migration
on the Rural Poor

Published in 2007 by ZUBAAN
K 92, Ist Floor, Hauz Khas Enclave
New Delhi 110016, India
Email: zubaanwbooks@vsnl.net / zubaan@gmail.com
Website: www.zubaanbooks.com

© Text: Smita (2006)
Photographs: Prashant Panjiar (2006)

ISBN 81 89884 17 4

Design: Uzma Mohsin, Visual Vibe
www.visualvibe.net

Printed at: Brijbasi Art Press, A 81, Sector 5, Noida

CONTENTS

FOREWORD

THE POOR IN INDIA suffer from a variety of tribulations and afflictions. They are all quite dreadful, but some of them are at least well understood and well analysed, so that remedies can be sought if we manage to get our act together. The fact that we do not seem often enough to be able to get our act together is, of course, true, but in dealing with such well-understood problems as widespread and chronic undernutrition, or lack of school facilities and basic health care, the task of the concerned citizen is well defined and suggests the need for more insistent political demand, public pressure and social agitation for economic and social expansion of the kind that would make a difference to these well-characterized deprivations. The practice of democracy demands that we get up and do something, rather than sit and hope that things will sort themselves out automatically. However, the nature of the problems and their possible solutions are at least well investigated and the possible remedies are, to a great extent, reasonably clear.

There is, however, another class of deprivations that have received so little concentrated attention that their basic features (including the magnitudes involved, the direct and indirect correlates and consequences of the primary problems, the nature of policy instruments that could make a real and effective difference) are shrouded in ignorance and confusion. One such problem is the huge phenomenon of what is called "distress seasonal migration". By making an important — and to some extent pioneering — contribution in analysing this miserable social phenomenon, the author of this study has taken a significant step in drawing attention to the nature, magnitude and the far-reaching consequences of this terrible state of affairs, which afflicts so many human lives in India, including a gigantic number of luckless children whose parents are forced to undertake distress seasonal migration. This prevents normal schooling, regular health care and basic social and civic attention coming to the children.

Two distinct aspects of "distress seasonal migration" need to be distinguished. There is, first and foremost, the issue of its magnitude and its causation. The phenomenon of migration is not in itself one of distress, but the result of terrible things that happen to people's lives, sometimes with great regularity. The migration itself is really an attempt to cope with those terrible things, through the only way available to the poor and the underprivileged to deal with local deprivation, to wit, going elsewhere in search of a less grim set of possibilities. There will be no way of eradicating "distress seasonal migration" unless the causes of such distress, which apparently have a pattern of seasonality, are themselves addressed and overcome. We can think of this as "the foundational task" which needs to be more fully worked out, and then — on the basis of better understanding — appropriately addressed.

The second aspect of the phenomenon includes the consequences of such migration and the adversities that the migration itself generates. Since the foundational task will not be completed overnight, we have to see how the adverse consequences of distress seasonal migration can be reduced, and where possible eliminated. We can think of this as "the immediate task."

This fine contribution is an attempt to deal with both these aspects of the tragic phenomenon of distress seasonal migration. The reader will find that the principal focus of this report is on the immediate task. This is, I think, the right focus for a pace-setting study of this kind. This is so for two distinct reasons. First, the foundational phenomenon is really an offshoot of rural poverty and social deprivation, and demands a much bigger research agenda to be linked with the huge literature that already exists on that broader subject. In contrast, the basic features of the immediate task raise questions that are quite specific, in the need to address the particular problems of children out of school, their being beyond the reach of immunization and standard health care, and so on. These features of distress seasonal migration have also been much more neglected and often have received next to no attention. There are, thus, excellent epistemic grounds for focusing on the clarification of the nature of the "immediate task" that is called for.

Second, even though the ultimate solution of the problem would demand massive action at a very wide level, integrated with the removal of rural poverty, deprivation and insecurity, there are things that can be done, even in the short run, to reduce the terrible effects of distress seasonal migration, especially on the children who are caught in their parents' battle for survival and the family's fight to keep alive. The immediate task has an urgency that links both with the severity of the proximate need and with the possibility of seeking temporary remedies, which may have to go on for many years, until the more basic foundational problem is resolved. There is, thus, an excellent practical reason for this concentration on the "immediate task," in addition to its epistemic importance.

This study is a fine beginning for a fuller understanding of the "immediate task," with some guidance also about the "foundational task" that lies behind it. Much more work will be needed on both the foundational and immediate tasks, but by undertaking this work, the author of this study has put us greatly in her debt.

Amartya Sen, Harvard University
Chair, AIF Advisory Council

Preface

INDIA HAS LONG had a commitment to the Universalization of Elementary Education (UEE). The Constitutional Amendmenon of 2005 that made elementary education a fundamental right further strengthened this. In 2002 the government set up the Sarva Shiksha Abhiyan (SSA), a flagship programme that aims to achieve UEE by 2010 and over the last decade and a half, considerable efforts have been made towards this end.

Not only has there been a perspective shift in policy but significant efforts have been made to take the school to the child who has been left out, instead of the other way round. A range of alternative and innovative options has been created to bring these children, who are out of the education net for various reasons, into the mainstream. Many complementary strategies with a provision of lateral entry into schools have been initiated to cover the existing backlog.

Despite this, children who are difficult to reach are still not receiving adequate attention from the State. While the booming Indian economy has provided tremendous opportunities of growth for the top 20 per cent of its population, those at the bottom have been further marginalized. This situation has given rise to new challenges that need to be continuously grappled with. One such challenge is the rising trend of 'distress seasonal migration', that is, millions of families being forced to leave their homes and villages for several months every year in search of livelihoods. These migrations mean that families are uprooted and their children are forced to drop out of school, something that closes up the only available opportunity to break this vicious cycle generation after generation. At work sites migrant children are inevitably put to work. All evidence indicates that migrations are large and growing. The number of children below 14 years of age thus affected, may already be in the order of 9 million.

The phenomenon of seasonal migration is highly complex, largely unresearched, and more or less ignored by all — be it the government, academia, the development sector or the media. In their drive for profits, and being away from mainstream scrutiny, employers have a free hand to exploit not only adult labourers but also their children in unthinkable ways, bypassing their legal and human obligations. Distress seasonal migration poses great challenges when it comes to interventions — one, because this phenomenon is complex and differs widely from sector to sector (with underlying common elements, however); two, because of the inherent instability in the lives of the migrants who do not stay in one place throughout the year but are on the move between villages and work sites.

This study was commissioned by American India Foundation (AIF) and draws from the work of four of its NGO partners, Janarth, working with sugarcane migrants in Maharashtra, Setu, the Centre for Social knowledge and Action, working with salt pan workers, charcoal makers and other migrants in Gujarat, Vikalpa and Lok Drishti working with brick kiln migrants from districts of Western Orissa to Andhra Pradesh. In 2003 AIF's work with children of seasonal migrants began with a chance interaction with Pravin Mahajan of Janarth on their 'sakharshala' intervention, that is, their work with children of migrants in sugarcane harvesting. Further engagement made it clear that what Janarth was addressing was just the tip of the iceberg. The problem extended far beyond those working only in sugarcane harvesting, nor was it limited only to Maharashtra, or indeed to running schools at migration sites. AIF's larger programme on education of children of seasonal migrants grew out of this understanding. While it was recognized that to mitigate the 'distress' of this type of migration, interventions were required on many fronts such as in the area of livelihoods, rights and entitlements, health, etc, AIF made education its entry point, with the aim of building contextualized models over a range of sectors and geographies, engaging with government to take the work to scale, and bringing this issue into the larger discourse.

This study tries to capture the macro as well as the micro picture of distress seasonal migration — covering the spread and scale of the occurrence, the seasonality factor, the differing contexts (geographies/sectors), the employer-labour relationships, the working and living conditions of migrant families and children, and how this type of migration promotes child labour. It also highlights the condition of schools in the sending areas and the overall response (or lack thereof) of the education system towards these children. The impact that migration has, year after year, on the lives of families and communities has also been explored. The study also deals with the disenfranchisement caused as people find themselves stripped of their basic rights and entitlements both at worksites and in their villages; and the response of the state/legal apparatus to their situation. This work deals specifically with migrations that are intra rural, and from rural to urban peripheries. Migration to cities and metros for work in the informal sector also manifests elements of distress, but that is not covered here.

The second part of the study describes the education programmes of the four NGOs, Janarth, Setu, Vikalpa and Lok Drishti, and presents the intervention model for education evolved over the last three years for comprehensive coverage of these children. Work in various states and sectors has enabled rich comparisons and contrasts. In addition, the study also identifies some of the gaps in research and policy, and suggests steps that can be taken to address these.

A literature survey has shown that while there are many valuable studies available on migration with respect to specific sectors and locations, there is not much that brings together experiences and lessons from across sectors and geographies. This study attempts to do that in order to be of help to academics, policy makers and development professionals.

distress seasonal migration: the annual trudge for survival

AN OVERVIEW

SINCE THE National Policy on Education (NPE) was introduced in 1986, a number of efforts have been made to achieve the goal of Universalization of Elementary Education (UEE). For the first time since independence, there has been a perspective shift in policy, and widespread attempts to actually implement it by reaching the school to the left-out child, instead of the other way round. This has been institutionalized through the Education Guarantee Scheme and Alternative Innovative Education ((EGS and AIE). Under the Sarva Shiksha Abhiyan children who are out of the education net for various reasons, or those who fall out of it, have been identified category wise, and a range of alternative and innovative options have been created for their coverage and mainstreaming. Many complementary strategies with a provision of lateral entry in schools have been initiated to cover the existing backlog.

Given this positive scenario, it has become imperative to continue to bring to light those most difficult groups of children who are yet to receive attention from the government, development agencies and others, so that the process does not stop until all children have actually been reached. While the booming Indian economy has provided tremendous opportunities of growth for the top 20 per cent of its population, those at the bottom have been further marginalized. This has given rise to many new challenges that need to be continuously grappled with. One such challenge is the rising trend of "distress seasonal migration" — tens of millions of families being forced to leave their homes and villages for several months every year, to head for locations near and far, in search of livelihood.

In these migrations families are also forced to take their children along. All evidence indicates that the number of migrant children below 14 years of age may already be of the order of 9 million. Before dwelling on children's education, however, it is important to reflect on the complex phenomenon of distress seasonal migration.

| DISTRESS SEASONAL MIGRATION: AN EMERGING PHENOMENON |

Seasonal migration has long been practised in rural areas for improving livelihood opportunities, with some male members of the family going out of their villages to look for better paid work, but in the last few decades there has been growing incidence of distress seasonal migration whereby drought and environmental degradation are forcing entire families to migrate in search of work merely to survive. Children also accompany their parents, drop out of schools, and are forced into hard labour.

Distress seasonal migration has been attributed as much to uneven development (National Commission on Rural Labour (NCRL), 1991) as to caste and social structure.[1] Large-scale distress seasonal migrations were triggered off in the late 60s by persistent drought in rainfall-deficit regions of the country. This coincided with the creation of irrigation facilities and commercial agriculture in surplus areas, resulting in high labour demand during specific seasons. Urbanization and infrastructure development in recent decades have also proved catalytic, with employers constantly and persistently reaching out for the unending supply of cheap labour from remote, impoverished pockets. The phenomenon however is becoming more complex with time, and increasingly, there are trends of local labour

1. See Mosse et al, 2002; Ravi Srivastava 2005

being displaced by migrant labour. Migrant labourers are more vulnerable and open to control. Thus the traditional causes for distress migration are getting interlocked with the employer's intent of labour control.

Migrant populations overwhelmingly belong to Scheduled Caste (SC), Scheduled Tribe (ST) and Other Backward Caste (OBC) categories. They comprise the landless and land poor who possess the least amount of assets, skills or education. Studies reveal that the majority of the migrant labour in states like Rajasthan, Karnataka, Gujarat, Andhra Pradesh, Tamil Nadu and Maharashtra are from the most marginalized sections of society (also see Srivastava, 2005).

| SECTORS THAT ATTRACT MIGRANT LABOUR |

Many industrial and agro-industrial sectors, like brick making, salt manufacture, sugar cane harvesting, stone quarrying, construction, fisheries, plantations, rice mills and so on, run largely on migrant labour. A high incidence of migrant labour is also found in the agriculture sector. Industrial migrations are for long periods of six to eight months and take place once a year. Agricultural migrations are for shorter durations of a few weeks and take place several times a year for operations such as sowing, harvesting and transplantation. Almost all major states appear to be affected by migration, although to varying degrees. The agriculturally and industrially developed states are likely to be the net receiving states for migrant labour, while the less developed states the net sending ones. Likewise there is also substantial intra state migration taking place. In addition, there is a complicated circulation of labour in evidence, which defies the surplus-deficit argument, and which is far from clearly understood today.

Almost all major states appear to be affected by migration, although to varying degrees.

The migration we talk about is not a journey with a destination, as in resettlement, but an ongoing process of mobility or labour circulation.

| THE SEASONAL MIGRATION CYCLE |

This type of labour mobility is seasonal, because of the uneven rhythm of economic activities over the year — peak periods alternating with slack periods — and also because of the open-air character of the production process, which makes it necessary for the work to stop with the onset of the monsoon. The entire operation is thus geared to this seasonality. Labour contractors provide cash advances to poor families in villages during the lean post-monsoon months, in return for which they pledge their labour for the coming season. Migrations begin between October and November; families spend the next six to eight months at worksites, returning to their villages by the next monsoon. Once the monsoon is over they again prepare to leave. Thus run the uprooted lives of tens of millions of the poorest rural families. The debt bondage that drives these migrations has been seen as a form of 'forced labour' by the International Labour Organisation (ILO), in which the element of compulsion is derived from debt. It has been argued that as the traditional system of bonded labour declined in the mid-90s, the steady supply of migrant labour gave rise to a new form of bondedness.[2]

The various operations of distress migration, starting from mobilization of the workforce by labour contractors in villages, to its transportation to distant worksites, and the production process at worksites, fall in the realm of the illegal. Living and working conditions of migrant labour at worksites are sub-minimal in every respect, whether it is shelter, nutrition, health or security. The work extracted from these labourers is excessive, and completely disproportionate to the payments made, which are far below the legal minimum wage. Women are also expected to measure up to men

in the physically arduous and exploitative work. Women and girls cope additionally with domestic responsibilities as well as the psychological insecurity of living in such unprotected environments. Their situation is therefore worse than that faced by those who live at home in their villages, who are also similarly marginalized. There are no mechanisms for redressing grievances. The basic clauses of all acts related to labour and child rights are flouted, raising exploitation levels to the extreme. Employers maximize their profits by maintaining their producers at bare survival levels. The legislation governing migration is grossly outdated, inadequate and poorly implemented (see below for more details on this).

The migration we talk about is not a journey with a destination, as in resettlement, but an ongoing process of mobility or labour circulation. The circulation is an outcome of the extension of scale of the labour market due to infrastructure development and an increase in transportation facilities, which makes bridging distances easier than in the past. In other words, this type of migration relates to the development process. People are not only driven out because of poverty but also because employers elsewhere, often far away, find it attractive to recruit them precisely because they are labour migrants which makes them more vulnerable. Labour migration is thus linked to local labour displacement — local labour is forced to move to other regions while a steady influx of labour nomads from elsewhere takes over. This is evident everywhere, even at the village level where a village landlord bypasses the local labourers if they demand full wages, getting cheap labour from outside, or the entire brick industry of a state which starts

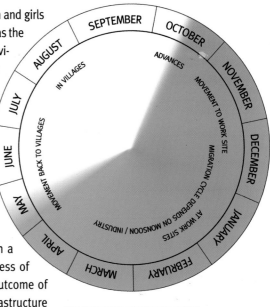

THE SEASONAL MIGRATION CYCLE

■ SEASONAL MIGRATION

2. See Ravi Srivastava (2005), Breman (1996)

This labour force is largely "invisible" as migration sites are located in remote areas.

accessing cheaper labour from tribal pockets far away, while local labour ends up looking for work in another region or state. This is slowly becoming the norm rather than an exception.

As Jan Breman argues,

The deprivation and degradation arising out of distress migration cannot be understood as the inevitable outcome of stagnation and backwardness. Its origin lies in the politics and policies of the development process itself... Contrary to the idea that poverty is a manifestation of economic redundancy, the down and out produce wealth from which they however remain excluded as beneficiaries.[3]

Distress migration is becoming the last coping strategy in the precarious lives of the rural poor. It has also become an inter-generational phenomenon, and it is common to come across fourth and even fifth generation migrants in many sectors.

DISTRESS MIGRANTS — THE MISSING CITIZENS

There is a stark absence of policy debate on the peculiar situation of migrant labour, who belong neither to their villages nor to their destination areas. They have to forego government welfare benefits in their villages, and are unable to access these at the migration sites. Migrant labour often cannot participate in elections and are not included in the census, thus becoming disenfranchised. This labour force is largely "invisible" as migration sites are located in remote areas, away from habitation, and mainstream public view. As Breman notes, "They build and sustain economies but are seen as being the perennial outsiders." Research on this subject is sparse[4] as is the reference to this

category of population in media and development discourse.

This dehumanised workforce enables huge profits for the sectors it supports, which are spent neither in making adequate payments to them nor in improving their conditions of work ...they are neither organized by trade unions nor protected by state legislation. They lack the social security that dignifies labour. (Breman, 2000)

3. Breman, Jan; Down and Out, Oxford University Press, New Delhi, 2000, pp19
4. Migration is only now catching the attention of scholars and media through activists and scholars like Jan Breman. Breman's extensive work since the early 80s is focused on human rights violations.

Although evidence throughout the country shows that the numbers involved in distress seasonal migrations are large and growing, there is little systematic data available. The two main secondary sources of data on population mobility in India are the Census and the National Sample Survey (NSS). But they do not adequately capture seasonal and circular migration due to empirical and conceptual difficulties. For example the definitions of migrants used in both surveys are not employment-related.[5] The NCRL has estimated, based on their data of industries employing migrant workers, that the number of seasonal and circular migrants is 10 million in rural areas alone. Of these an estimated 4.5 million are inter state migrants. Other informal estimates put the total number closer to 30 million.[6] Small-scale studies provide some regional and sector wise estimates. But these are sundry pieces of the jigsaw puzzle, while the larger picture is far from clear. With regard to the child population in distress family migrations, there is fairly widespread field evidence[7] that children accompanying their parents in the 0-14 age group may constitute about a third of the total migrant population, and those in the elementary school age group (6-14 years) about 20 per cent, or 6 million.[8] These are conservative estimates, and the reality may well surpass this.

Data gaps lead to policy gaps. In the absence of a proper database on the extent and scale of distress seasonal migration, and its impact on families as well as communities, the issue is unlikely to find a place in the policy discourse and, therefore, the planning framework. Today seasonal migrants are not recognized as a category to be addressed in the country's development planning, unlike tribals and dalits. Seasonal migrants belong to the poorest sections of the population, and represent the major and growing phenomenon of labour mobility driven by a livelihood collapse in rural areas,[9] which the government needs to recognize as a looming challenge. Despite this, they are not reflected in the Five Year Plans, nor are they the focus of any special schemes or sub-plans, thus remaining bereft of any vehicle for change.

SEASONAL MIGRATION AND EDUCATION PLANNING

Distress migration is an insidious promoter of child labour. NCRL too notes a high incidence of child labour in a number of sectors.

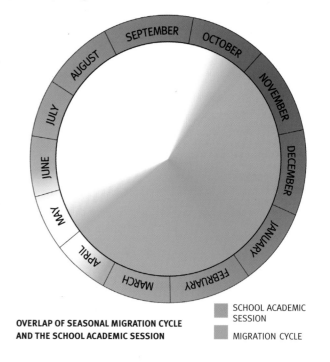

OVERLAP OF SEASONAL MIGRATION CYCLE AND THE SCHOOL ACADEMIC SESSION

SCHOOL ACADEMIC SESSION

MIGRATION CYCLE

5. Firstly, definitions of migrants used in both surveys (change from birthplace and change in last usual place of residence), are not employment related. Secondly, migration surveys give only the main reason for migration, and that too at the time of migration. Another problem is that migration data relate to stocks of migrants and not to flows, although different policy concerns relate to stocks (of different ages) and flows.

6. Discussions in 'National Consultation on Social Security for Migrant Workers in the Informal Sector' organised by DFID and ILO, N. Delhi, August 2005.

7. Although impressionistic, based on small-scale studies and field evidence across many sectors and geographies.

8. In informal discussion with Prof Jan Breman, Ravi Srivastava and Priya Deshingkar.

9. See recent writings of P. Sainath.

Poor families with no backup support in their villages, have little recourse but to take their children along. At worksites, the employer, contractor or the parents invariably draw the small hands and feet into the labour process. This is due to the nature of wage payment, which is on a piece rate basis rather than on hours of work. The vulnerability of migrant children is aggravated since being out of their domain they are cut off from care and security, health and nutrition, learning and exposure, and an overall normalcy of childhood, things that are better assured within a stable home, and which non-migrant children living in the village experience as a matter of course. Needless to say that among migrant children, the girl child suffers the most. There is very little that we can say today about the possible detrimental effects on the future lives of children born or raised on worksites.

The status of government schools in migration prone regions is found to be dismal. These remote and backward regions have governance much below the state average, and the school system is no exception. Even in progressive states like Maharashtra and Gujarat, in the high-migration pockets, which lie in the backward districts, school functioning is less than satisfactory. Poor education possibilities push children further into migration. Ironically, with large-scale enrolment drives, the names of most migrant children are on school rolls; but in reality they are out of school, getting sucked into labour at worksites, and falling irreversibly into the vicious annual cycle.

Why is education critical to the issue of distress seasonal migration? Because the window of opportunity that children of migrant families have is very small. They get drawn into labour early, and are usually full-fledged labourers by the age of 11 or

12. They face a life of hardship and a sense of displacement right from infancy. They are subjected to hazardous travel between villages and work sites, and a life of severe deprivation at the latter. Girl children endure many more deprivations than boys. It is well known that they receive less nutrition and less care than boys, and often have to do double the work, at work sites as well as at home. But migrant girls also have to deal with the fact of

Among migrant children, the girl child suffers the most.

24

The country is striving towards Millennium Development Goals. Despite this little attention is given to the plight of migrant families.

being female, and having female bodies. Parents do not like to leave grown-up girls behind in the villages as they may do boys, but at work sites and in unprotected environments girls are constantly subjected to sexual abuse.

In villages, these children find acceptance neither in school nor in the larger community, and are constantly viewed as outsiders. Moreover, such children are elusive, and difficult to trace, therefore easily left out of the standard systemic interventions. Even many of the alternative schooling innovations may not fit the bill because of their mobility. But clearly, it is important that this vicious cycle be broken. Unless proper educational opportunities are ensured for these children and unless they are rigorously pursued, they will be forced to make the Hobson's choice their parents made.

India is in the process of implementing the Right to Education Act 2005. The country is striving towards Millennium Development Goals (MDGs), of which the second talks of achieving universal primary education by 2015. And through the much more ambitious Sarva Shiksha Abhiyan (SSA) the Indian government is working to achieve Universalization of Elementary Education (UEE) by 2010. The country is also signatory to the UN Child Rights Charter (1999). Ironically, despite this positive scenario, little attention is given to the plight of the children of migrant labour. Year after year their ranks are swelling. But the Ministry of Human Resource Development and the state education departments lack even the basic awareness and data with respect to this category of children, nor do they have a strategic plan in place for their coverage. Unless urgent steps are taken for their education and development needs, we will fail to meet UEE targets and the MDGs.

THE CONTOURS AND DYNAMICS OF DISTRESS SEASONAL MIGRATION

S EASONAL FAMILY migrations are now widespread, but not well understood or documented. Any attempt to grasp the reality of this phenomenon inevitably leads the researcher into a number of complex and inter-related issues. It is impossible to focus on children without, for example, studying the whole gamut of issues that define distress seasonal migrations, such as the spread and scale of the occurrence, the differing geographical and sectoral contexts, the seasonality factor, the employer-labour relationships, and so on. A holistic understanding of the scenario is essential to make effective interventions in policy and practice. This section deals with the broad contours of distress seasonal migration, and tries to capture some of its critical dynamics.

| CATEGORIZING SEASONAL MIGRATION |

Migrations can be categorized according to various parameters:
> Nature of industry/work
   Partially organized/unorganized
   Agricultural/industrial/agro industrial
> Duration of migration
   Short (4-8 weeks)/long (6-8 months) /round the year
> Distance of migration
   Intra district/inter district/inter state
> Destination of migration
   Intra rural
   Rural – urban peripheries
   Rural – urban centres
> Who migrates
   Male migration/family migration/child migration
> Purpose of migration
   For accumulation/for survival

DEFINING 'DISTRESS SEASONAL MIGRATION'

It is important to distinguish migrations for accumulation from those for survival or those that occur because of distress. While the former are by choice, usually undertaken by able-bodied males of the family, involve a basic negotiation ability on the part of the migrants, and enable investment in asset creation, the latter fail to display any of the above characteristics. Three elements which appear to characterize distress seasonal migration, are:

1. A lack of alternatives in sending areas which forces entire families, including children, to migrate in search of work, a nd pushes children into hazardous labour and the vicious migration cycle
2. Work which is based on debt bondedness, generates little or no surplus for the labourer at the end of the season, and is merely for survival
3. Work which involves large-scale violation of labour laws and child rights

| KEY FEATURES |

Some of the key features of the phenomenon of distress seasonal migration are discussed below:

It is important to distinguish migrations for accumulation from those for survival.

| THE CAUSES OF MIGRATION |

A major push factor which triggers distress migration is the lack of livelihood options in rain fed areas, in various parts of the country, particularly after the monsoon (kharif) crop. The consequent indebtedness and food insecurity forces large numbers to migrate in search of work. The reasons vary from place to place, but stem from persistent drought, land and environmental degradation, salinity ingress in coastal areas, displacement due to large-scale mining, mega dams, heavy industry, etc. Together with inter-regional disparity, variations in development policy also play a role.

The pull factors include high seasonal demand for manual labour in agriculturally advantaged areas, as well as labour intensive industries such as salt manufacture, brick making, sugarcane harvesting, stone quarrying etc. These sectors are characterized by a predominance of manual processes, seasonality, remoteness, work done out in the open and contract labour.

| TYPES AND PATTERNS OF MIGRATION |

Agriculture based migrations are of short duration. These may take place several times a year with families making 4-8 week trips for sowing, harvesting or transplantation. There are variations in pattern depending on the crop.[10] The migrations are diverse, usually short distance and highly scattered, and the migrants difficult to trace since they wander around in small groups of one or a few families. Industrial, agro-industrial and related migrations, such as brick-making, salt manufacture, tile-making, fisheries-based migrations, stone quarrying, construction, charcoal-making, sugarcane harvesting, work at rice mills, etc., have a single cycle of 6-8 months per year. These migrations begin after the monsoon around November, and end the next year between April and June. The families live in large camps or bivouacs near work sites during the migration period. When they return to their villages, if there is adequate rain, those who own some land try to eke out a crop from it, while the landless find work on farms. In the event of a monsoon failure, everyone in the village faces food shortage which leads to a general sense of insecurity for a few months.

Situations on the ground, however, are not as neat as this. Migration periods for those living in extreme poverty may become longer; also employers

10. For example the regular rabi and kharif crops require labour twice a year, rice four times a year, coffee plantations for two months in a year, cotton for four and so on.

MIGRATION CIRCUITS

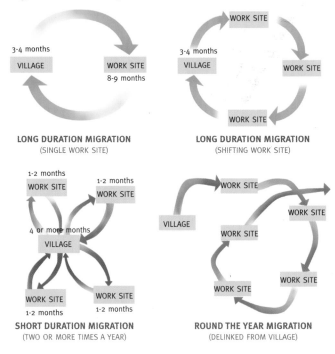

*Distress migration is triggered
by the lack of livlihood options
in rain fed areas.*

With increasing abject poverty, employers are accessing cheap labour from remote, agriculturally distressed areas.

11. Information from Santulan, a Maharashtra based NGO working with stone quarry migrants.

12. 'Short term migration in south Rajasthan - Incidence and Impact', Sudhir Katiyar, Sudrak, 2005 (draft report).

13. States: Rajasthan, UP, Bihar, MP, Maharashtra, West Bengal, Orissa, AP, Kerala; Sectors: Salt pans, Sugarcane cutting, roof tiles, construction, fish processing, brick kilns, loading - unloading, power-loom, diamond polishing, cotton pollination, cotton ginning mills, sari folding, small scale industries.

14. Bolangir, Kalahandi, Bargarh, Sonepur and Koraput.

often try to retain some labour round the year. Many migrant families are forced to trudge from one type of work to another to clear accumulated debt. In extreme cases there is evidence of families being completely uprooted from their villages, and on the move round the year, going from one work site to another. The stone quarries in parts of Maharashtra[11] and Uttar Pradesh have begun to operate round the year. They have installed technology to pump water out of the quarries during the monsoon. Thus, more and more families who migrate for stone quarrying are not returning to their villages, and settling down at the work sites. They can no longer be called 'seasonal migrants' as there is no seasonality in this work any more. The distressful living conditions at stone quarries, although they provide year round employment, throw up their own set of challenges.

The most insidious migrations are the child-only migrations[12] prevalent in the cottonseed production sector in Andhra Pradesh, Gujarat and Karnataka. This sector employs children, mainly girls. A substantial number of children are migrants and leave their homes for three to four months every year (July-October). The migrations happen within Andhra Pradesh and from south Rajasthan to north Gujarat. This trend is surfacing in other places too — the city of Hyderabad, for example, where agents bring only children from neighbouring districts to perform certain functions at construction sites.

It is pertinent to also mention the pastoral migrations common in the western parts of Rajasthan and Gujarat comprising the desert districts. Sheep, goat and camel rearing are the traditional occupations here, and several communities like the Raikas and Maldharis move for some months every year in pre-defined circular routes for the purpose of grazing their flocks. Similarly there are the Van Gujars of Uttaranchal who move with their animals between the upper and lower reaches of the mountains. These migrations are part of age-old occupational practices of pastoral communities, and while the question of education is equally relevant for their children, they are not dealt with here.

| MAPPING MIGRATION |

Data suggests that distress seasonal migration is likely to be a reality in a large number of states. The National Human Rights Commission Expert Group (2000) found a high incidence of migrant bonded labour in states like Bihar, Jharkhand, Chattisgarh, Tamil Nadu, Madhya Pradesh, Orissa, Rajasthan, Punjab and Haryana. Various other information sources show a high incidence of it in Maharashtra, Gujarat, Andhra Pradesh, West Bengal and other states as well.

Migration takes place intra state as well as inter state. The poorer states tend to be the 'net sending states' (e.g. Orissa, Bihar) while the industrialized, agriculturally rich ones the 'net

We came across some small communities from Ajmer region of Rajasthan, who were originally performing artists, but having lost their livelihood, they have turned into impoverished labour nomads - they spend some months in charcoal making in local areas, following which they go to Delhi to beg on the streets, and then return to their villages around the monsoon for a few months. We met a group of pastoral migrants in Maharashtra, who were Bharwars from Gujarat. They told us that they had been moving with their animals for the last 15 years. Their only connection left with their village in Surendranagar district was their temple, to which some male members go annually to pay their respects.

receiving states' (e.g. Gujarat, Punjab). Gujarat alone receives labourers from about nine states, for work in over a dozen sectors.[13] A similar scenario is evident in states with deficit areas sending labour to surplus areas. For instance, within Gujarat large-scale migration takes place from tribal districts Dahod and Panchmahal to a dozen other districts.

While migration has all along been seen as an optional activity, the last few decades have seen this perception change. With increasing incidence of abject poverty in some parts, employers have begun to proactively access cheap labour from remote, agriculturally distressed areas, particularly drylands and forest areas that have witnessed continuing exploitation. Tribal areas are being especially targeted. In this drive for cheap labour, employers easily cross state boundaries and arrange to transport tens of thousands of labourers across long distances to their work sites. A classic case is the western Orissa to Andhra Pradesh brick kiln migrations in which 100,000-150,000 labourers are moved from the four to five tribal districts[14] across 600-800 kilometres by train.

There is also a clear trend of local labour being displaced by migrant labour, because of the greater vulnerability of the latter to financial, physical and other exploitation.

There is evidence of labour from one district in Gujarat going to another district, while local labour from that district goes to a third district. Similarly, labour from Andhra Pradesh finds employment in Karnataka brick kilns as labour from Orissa displaces them in their own state. Inward migration of labour in some areas is sometimes matched by outward migration.[15] The NCRL has also noted the phenomenon of the same region both supplying and importing migrant labour. These trends have resulted in widespread depression of wages and disempowerment of labour.

In a field visit to tribal Madhya Pradesh we found that when a group of Sahariya tribals in Shivpuri district who were underpaid workers on nearby farms got together to demand for minimum wages, they were left without work as the landowner arranged for cheaper labour from elsewhere.

This complicated circulation of labour among and within states, is far from clearly understood. There is an urgent need to map these migration flows and study the patterns and trends in order to understand migration better.

| THE MAGNITUDE OF MIGRATION |

Estimates of migration, including child migration have been arrived at in the following sectors and geographies:

SUGARCANE MIGRATIONS, MAHARASHTRA

Maharashtra produces about 70 per cent of the sugar in the country, with a total of 186 cooperative sugar factories. Large-scale sugarcane cultivation began here in the early 70s after the Koina dam was built. The seven districts in western Maharashtra — Nasik, Ahmadnagar, Pune, Satara, Sangli, Kolhapur and Sholapur — comprise the sugar belt, which extends into Surat (Gujarat) in the north and Belgaum (Karnataka) in the south. Five districts of the arid Marathwada region — Beed, Jalgaon, Ahmadnagar, Nasik and Jalna — send out labour to this sugar belt for six months every year for sugarcane harvesting.

A study commissioned by Janarth, an Aurangabad-based NGO, estimates that about 650,000 labourers migrate from central to western Maharashtra for sugarcane cutting each year.[16] Of these around 200,000 are children in the elementary school age group of 6-14 years. An additional 200,000 labourers are received in Surat district of Gujarat for sugarcane cutting every season, of which 75 per cent are from Khandesh region of Maharashtra, and the rest from Dangs and other tribal districts in Gujarat. Estimates of migration into Belgaum put it in the range of 100,000 per season.

15. Also see Srivastava, 1998
16. By Centre of Development Research and Documentation (CDRD), Nashik; 2003.

An estimated 650,000 labourers migrate for sugarcane cutting of which 200,000 are children of 6-14 years.

BRICK KILN MIGRATIONS, WESTERN ORISSA TO ANDHRA PRADESH

According to ActionAid estimates approximately 200,000 people migrate from predominantly tribal western Orissa districts[17] to brick kilns on the periphery of some major cities of Andhra Pradesh,[18] which are reportedly illegal. From Bolangir district alone 100,000 to 150,000 people migrate every year. A child is an essential part of the work unit that the contractors hire for brick work in Orisssa. A study of 300 brick kilns around Hyderabad revealed that as many as 35 per cent of the total migrants comprised children, of which 22 per cent were in the school going age of 6-14 years. While the bulk of this migration is to Andhra Pradesh, some is also to Mumbai, Surat, Varanasi, Raipur and other cities to work on construction sites, in weaving units and hotels, and as rickshaw pullers.

According to the All India Brick Kilns and Tile Manufacturer's Federation there are around 50,000 brick kilns in India, each employing on an average 100 permanent workers. These alone amount to a total of 5 million workers in the kilns. However, only the male heads of the family are registered as workers on the rolls. Taking a conservative estimate of five members per family, a staggering figure of 25 million is obtained as those dependent on the brick sector for their livelihoods, a third of which are likely to be children.

SALT PAN AND OTHER MIGRATIONS, GUJARAT

Gujarat produces 66 per cent of the salt in India in inland and marine salt pans. Marine salt pans dot a quarter of the 1600 kilometre coastline of the state.[19] Kutchh is the major salt district, producing 60 per cent of the total salt in the state. Salt is pro-

duced in inland salt pans in the Little Rann of Kutchh, by drawing out saline ground water, and in marine salt pans along the coastline, using salty seawater. Setu, based in Ahemdabad, has undertaken an overview of migrations in Gujarat based on secondary data. According to them, an estimated 200,000 to 225,000 people migrate to Kutchh every year for salt making. Salt is also produced in 12 other districts of the state. These together are home to over 1600 salt producing units.

Apart from the salt sector, labour migration takes place in multiple sectors in Gujarat and all its 25 districts are affected by it. Over 100,000 families, or 500,000 individuals, migrate out of tribal districts Dahod, Panchmahal, and neighbouring Jhabua (in Madhya Pradesh) to over 13 districts of the state mainly for agriculture and construction work. Overall, an estimated 1.2 to 1.4 million people migrate or circulate within the state for work in the informal sector. This includes an influx of about 150,000 people from tribal Nandurbar and Dhule districts in Maharashtra and significant numbers from tribal Madhya Pradesh and Rajasthan and other states.[20]

OTHER MIGRATIONS

Stone quarrying is one of the biggest sectors attracting migrant labour. Almost 30 out of the 45 districts of the state are home to intensive stone quarrying, Vidarbha and western Maharashtra being the major-stone rich regions. According to Santulan, a Pune-based NGO, there are 4-5 million workers in this sector in Maharashtra alone of which 800,000-1,000,000 are likely to be children.

Cottonseed production is another sector that used to run on local labour. But with expansion, and the entry of multinational

17. Bolangir, Nuapada, Kalahandi, Bargarh, Sonepur.
18. 'From Hunger to Suffering', ActionAid, 2005.
19. Four major companies - Tata Salt, Gujarat Heavy Chemicals, Reliance and Nirma - run their operation on this coastline.
20. An overview of Migration in Gujarat, Setu (unpublished).

Of the different shapes and forms that migrations take, there is another variety to be seen in parts of Tamil Nadu.[21] In the coastal district of Cuddalore, a dalit village called Ambedkarnagar serves as a good illustration for what is the nature of this migration. Traditionally the families living here must have served as a labour pool for the main Hindu village some distance away. But these days income in the village is not much and more and more people are earning from jobs located outside. They retain a foot in the village for five months in a year working in the fields and fishing in the brackish backwaters, but for the remaining seven months they go for short trips to different places outside, depending on work availability. The work is usually on construction sites, in factories, and on cashew or casuarina plantations. Family members may go one or two at a time, do the available work outside the village and then return, only to go again sometime later. Several such trips may be made in a year by different family members. Clearly these migrations are very uncertain and highly disruptive of family life.

21. Venkateswarlu D (2005), 'Unilever and child labour in hybrid cottonseed production in Andhra Pradesh - Allegations and response', study commissioned by ActionAid, United Kingdom

22. In informal conversation with Priya Deshingkar.

23. Vanjaris, Marathas, Dhangars, Mangs and Mahars.

24. Vasava, Gamit, Kathud and Bhil.

25. Koli, Vaghri (STs), Mehgwal (SCs), Rabari and Bharwad (OBCs) GJJS estimates,1992-93.

26. Survey of 7 blocks by CADMB (Community Action Against Drought Mitigation in Bolangir) in Bolangir.

27. Janarth Sending Villages - A Survey Report, NCAS, 2005

companies in the 90s, the labour requirement went up, and both child labour and migrant child labour increased greatly in this sector. An estimated 450,000 children between the ages of 6-14 work in cottonseed production in the country, 250,000 of these are in AP and the rest in Gujarat and Karnataka.[22] Girls constitute 85 per cent of the work force in AP. They earn 30 per cent less than a woman and 55 per cent less than a man. Girls are preferred over boys in cotton pollination work, because traditionally it was women's work, and as the labour requirement increased, the work started to be passed on to girls. Almost a third of the child labourers in AP are migrants. In the last three years the prevalence of drought has brought commercial cottonseed production in AP down by 44 per cent and production is now shifting to Gujarat and Karnataka.

The cotton pollination child-only migrations from Rajasthan to north Gujarat run in huge numbers. Children from 8 years upwards are recruited from a large arc of tribal blocks on the border of south Rajasthan, spanning Sirohi, Udaipur and Dungarpur districts. An overall 44 per cent of these are girls, and in some areas girls outnumber boys. The total requirement of labour for the pollination season has been estimated at 3 lakh, to meet which recruitment is extending further inwards into Rajasthan as well as to the tribal areas of Gujarat.

| SOCIO-ECONOMIC PROFILE OF MIGRANTS |

The socio-economic background of migrants is similar across states: they come from the most marginalized and impoverished sections of society — Scheduled Castes (SCs), Scheduled Tribes (STs) and Other Backward Castes (OBCs). Studies show that an estimated 45 per cent sugarcane migrants within Maharashtra are OBCs , 15 per cent SCs, 28 per cent STs.[23] The migration from Maharashtra to Gujarat is almost entirely of tribals.[24] Of the salt migrants in Gujarat about half are STs, another one third SCs and the rest OBCs.[25] In Bolangir, Orissa, 38 per cent migrants are OBC, 20 per cent STs and 40 per cent SCs.[26] A majority of migrants are landless or land poor. They are also largely without assets, unskilled and illiterate. A survey[27] of sugarcane migrants in 165 sending villages in four districts of Maharashtra done by Janarth shows that:

> 40 per cent families were found to be landless; 32 per cent owned 1-2 acres of land

> 73 per cent families possessed BPL (Below Poverty Line) cards. (Over 12 per cent did not possess any ration cards)

> 66 per cent men and 92 per cent women were illiterate.

The dominant age profile of migrant labour is 21-40 years. The above study revealed that in this age group 94 per cent people migrate. But older and younger people also accompany, and contribute to family labour. Significantly, even among those above 60 years, 20 per cent are forced to migrate, and engage in hard labour. There are instances of women migrating alone from women-headed households. These migrants work at even more compromised levels of earning as compared to the 'able bodied'. Among children, in the 0-5 year age group, as expected, 85 per cent are taken. Significantly, up till 10 years of age nearly equal numbers of boys and girls migrate, but as the age increases more girls migrate than boys. According to parents, they do not want to risk leaving girls in the village without male protection. In most migrations it is largely the old, ill and the disabled who are left behind in the villages.

| DIFFERENTIATIONS IN MIGRATION |

Even in the realm of 'distress' there are differentiations. These are on account of factors such as caste, region, economic status, skill, experience, type of work, age, etc. Some sectors are preferred over others. Those of higher castes, and possessing better skills, assets and physical strength are able to secure work in sectors that are more organized, at higher advances, with more stable work conditions. Others may have to settle for lower advances, shifting work sites, and so on. They may have to change sectors frequently and be prepared for more unpredictability in general. Muslims, and people of lower castes may not even be allowed entry into some sectors.

While this differentiation is prevalent everywhere, it is most clearly illustrated in the Maharashtra sugar migrations. There are

A child is an essential part of the work unit that the contractors hire for brick work in Orissa.

In Beed district of Maharashtra when we followed a truck in which some families of sugarcane cutters were returning home at the end of the season, we found that next to their village were large brick kilns run on migrant labour. But these families would not deign to work in them, choosing instead to travel 300 kilometres away to sugarcane sites. According to them brickmaking was the work of dalits and muslims, while they were Marathas (a higher caste).

28. Tyre centre migrants bring their bullocks and are provided technologically improved carts (with rubber tyres) to transport sugarcane; They live in large settlements closer to the factory; the gadi centre migrants bring their own wooden bullock carts and animals and live further away from the factory; the doki centre migrants are mobile, they have no assets, they cut cane and load it into factory trucks, stay farthest away, work in groups of 15-20, and are shifted from site to site depending on cane availability and factory schedule.

three distinct categories of sugarcane cutters — the tyre centre workers, the gadi centre workers and the doki centre workers.[28] The tyre and gadi centre work is dominated by Vanjaris followed by Marathas who are of a higher caste and economic status. They possess bullocks that enable them to work in tyre and gadi centres. They live in pucca houses and have better education levels. Many from this category even make arrangements to keep one or two children back in their villages to go to school. The study cited above shows the proportion of such children to be as high as 41 per cent. The doki centre workers on the other hand are mainly SCs, STs and Muslims. They do not have bullocks or other assets. They work on lower advances, move on trucks and tractors with contractors, work in smaller groups, shift work sites every few weeks, and face far tougher work conditions than their counterparts in tyre and gadi centres. With hardly any backup support in villages, their children have no opportunity to go to school.

Not enough work has been done on caste profiles across and within migration sectors, although such a study is necessary and would be useful. Brick making, for instance, appears to be done largely by dalits and tribals. In brick making, people from certain caste groups and regions perform certain operations. For instance, brick moulders are from the lowest socio-economic strata and are also the least paid. In the salt sector in Gujarat, the entire set of skilled operations related to the crystallization of salt is carried out by the agariyas, the traditional salt makers. They are OBCs and belong to the Koli community. Unskilled jobs like taking salt out of the pans, its washing, loading and unloading, may be done by other castes as well. The construction sector in Gujarat runs mainly on tribals and dalits and charcoal making, the lowest ranked sector, runs mainly on dalits and muslims.

RECRUITMENT OF LABOUR

In some types of migrations workers move from their villages to work areas, based on information from kinship groups or through 'nakas' or labour markets. Repeated migrations help them build direct links with employers. In other types of migrations contractors engaged by employers recruit labour from source villages. The contractors in turn have sub contractors or agents or 'jobbers' at the village level. Contractors (mukaddams, sardars, seths, etc) advance money to migrant families in the post monsoon period, in return for the pledge of their labour for the ensuing season. A work unit usually comprises a man and a woman. In brick migrations in Orissa, however, the work unit comprises a man, a woman and a child (who is more or less unpaid)! These units go by different names — the sugarcane unit is called a 'koyata' (after the sickle used to cut cane), the Orissa brick unit is a 'pathar'; ten or twelve work units form a labour gang. At the work site the contractor supervises the work of the gang, and is responsible for their payments. In these labour gangs only the adult males are registered on the muster rolls, women are usually not. In addition several unpaid hands, especially children, are also forced into work, but remain invisible and unaccounted for.

The choice of a destination is not in the hands of migrants. They depend on the contractor's choice. Therefore migrant families may end up in different areas/work sites each year. In Orissa brick migration workers move 'in the blind', with no knowledge of where they are going. And with no village or habitation near work sites, often they never find out where they are. While in some migrations people from one village move and live together at work sites, Orissa brick migrations are reminiscent

of the slave trade, with community groups and even families being split up and sent to different destinations, thus depriving people of this most basic psychological security.

Families can also change contractors although this is not so straightforward, as contractors ensure their work units remain in their debt. If there is a change, the family has to ensure that the next contractor pays off the debt to the previous one. At times families may even be forced to change their sector of work, when demand for labour dips in their usual sector.

In interstate migrations the layers of middlemen increase. These networks are widespread, arranged hierarchically, and appear to work with great efficiency. Agents are usually former migrants (who made their way up the ladder through their enterprise), or even moneylenders.

Malpractice of all kinds is entrenched in these migrations. There is no labour registration, no contract letter stating terms of work, no insurance cover. The Maharashtra survey cited above shows that only 0.13 per cent of the surveyed migrants had a written document.

| LABOUR MOVEMENT FROM VILLAGES TO WORK SITES |

Travel conditions between villages and work sites are hazardous, especially in long distance migrations. Migrants generally carry with them an initial supply of grain and some provisions, utensils, bedding, clothes, even chickens and goats. Many sugarcane migrants of Maharashtra take their bullocks along as well. Some migrations may be short distance, and confined within the block or district, or at most within neighbouring districts. This is usually the case in agricultural migrations. Sugarcane migrants cross several

districts and make a journey of 200-300 kilometres on trucks arranged by agents, or in assorted public transport over 2-3 days, or on personal bullock carts over a week to ten days. Orissa brick migrants cross state boundaries and go into Andhra Pradesh. They are taken by agents on a 36-hour train journey to Hyderabad. It is a bizarre and inhuman sight with train bogies filled to four or five times their capacity. People are crushed to such an extent that they

There is no labour registration, no contract letter stating terms of work, no insurance cover.

cannot eat, drink or use the toilet. Suffocation deaths have been reported. Women and specially children are the worst sufferers in this process. All transportation costs have to be borne by the migrants. While short distance migrants have the advantage of being able to visit their homes in between, long distance migrants get cut off from their villages for the entire migration period.

| THE FINANCIAL ARRANGEMENTS |

Employers advance money to labour contractors to deliver a given amount of work. Contractors in turn recruit labour by advancing money to poor families in the post monsoon harvest period when their need for cash is greatest. In return for this, families pledge their labour for the entire season, entering into debt bondage. With this money they fulfil their urgent family needs like purchase of grain, medical treatment, marriage, repairs, the festival season, etc., and then prepare to migrate for the ensuing 6-8 months. The advance amounts are small, in the range of a few thousand rupees[29] per work unit, comprising two adults who are counted and 2-3 more pairs of hands, mostly children, who are not counted. The advance amounts are determined by the amount of work a family can offer during a season, judged by contractors on factors such as age, physical strength (with women and younger men/ boys counted as less productive), experience, length of season, family need and earlier debt. The transactions are unwritten, and controlled entirely by employers/contractors, with migrants having no negotiating power at all.

At work sites payments are made by piece rate,[30] which pulls every family member into work including small children. Of these the contractor retains a part to clear advances and he gives a small allowance to the family for its consumption needs

(at bare survival level). For any additional needs, like sickness or an emergency at home, the contractor keeps advancing money to his labourers, to be settled at the end of the season. All accounts remain with the contractor. At the time of final payments, taking advantage of their illiteracy he exploits the labourers in various ways — by showing a shortfall in production, misrepresenting accounts, withholding or delaying payments — and ultimately pays them way below what is their due. Moreover several types of deductions are made — travel costs, cost of shelter, hire charges for implements or carts given by the

29. Rs 5,000-10,000 in Orissa to AP brick migrations, ActionAID
Rs 3,500-5,000 in Gujarat salt migrations, Setu
Rs 10,000-25,000 in Maharashtra sugar migrations, Janarth.

30. Per 1000 bricks, per tonne of cane cut or salt produced.

employer, repair charges etc. Migrants also have to make other payments like shop credit. At the end the families are left with hardly any amount to take home and tide over the next few months in the village. Many end up getting into further debt with the contractor, to pay off which they have to find more work on the way back or borrow from the moneylender or pledge work for the next season. Piece rate payments and family labour make it impossible to ascertain exact daily earnings of labourers, but in all cases they are considerably below the minimum wage. Employers get away from minimum wage regulations by using this piece-rate approach.

What then makes these migrations take place year after year, from the viewpoint of the family as well as the employer? Clearly this system of contract labour, cash advances and piece-rate payments forms the economic basis for distress seasonal migrations, and is weighted totally in favour of the employers. The system whereby employers advance money to labour contractors for a given amount of work relieves them of any responsibility towards the labour force that produces this work, or "frees the owners of capital from the obligations of employer" (Breman,1996). The contractors who, in turn, advance money to poor families, use this debt as an instrument of control not only to extract inordinate amounts of work out of them, but also to tie them into relationships of dependence by offering patronage in unknown places far away from their homes, and the assurance of similar work, however exploitative, year after year. In this way contractors become the most intimate 'benefactors' as well as exploiters of their own community. Distress migration creates long term indebtedness for families, fails to generate cash returns and perpetuates below subsistence level livelihoods. (Also see Mosse, 2005). Another insidious

The inherent uncertainty in migration due to seasonal and market fluctuations impacts work availability.

aspect of this system is that it denies labourers any possibilities of upward mobility. It is not unusual to come across migrants who have been on the move for 25-30 years at the lowest paid unskilled levels, just as their families have done for two generations before them, and as their children will inevitably do in future, unless of course steps are taken to address the situation.

It needs to be underlined that because payment is on a piece rate basis — the more the production, the more the earning — the whole family gets involved. The employer does not 'employ children' as such, but the economic arrangement coerces families into putting all hands to work to increase production.

| UNCERTAINTIES AND INSTABILITIES |

There is inherent uncertainty involved in migration — seasons may vary in length depending on climatic conditions, market demands fluctuate and this impacts work availability. In Gujarat which is repeatedly hit by cyclones, the ceasing of salt pan work makes families look for work in other sectors. In Maharashtra, a strike by the sugarcane cooperatives in 2005 delayed the starting of the factories, and migrants who had arrived at the sites had to wait 3-4 weeks at their own expense for the work to begin. In a low demand season, it is the poorest of the poor who are seen to migrate. At a more micro level, a specific employer may close down or reduce operations, laying off the labour. In this eventuality, migrants who have not yet cleared their advances, have to find work elsewhere or get deeper into debt. While migrant labour is left to fend for itself industry, on the other hand, collectively negotiates for tax holidays, excise exemptions, subsidized fuel etc. to tide over unforeseen eventualities.[31]

At the supply end good rainfall in the source villages creates

> At a sugarcane site we met with a group of a 20-25 women and a bunch of children of various ages. The only male present was the contractor. Initially we were given the impression that things were as usual at this doki centre adda. The contractor and his wife were trying to make sure not to let us have any time separately with the women. But slowly we were able to piece together what the contractor was trying to hide from us - due to early closure of work in that factory the families had not been able to pay off the advance, therefore he was keeping the women 'captive' while the men had left the site a few days back to go and arrange for money.

more work locally, and less people migrate, conversely bad drought conditions step up migration. In the field areas of Setu, the rate is seen to vary between 25 and 35 per cent. Similarly, the variation is in the range of 30 per cent in Vikalpa's field areas, another AIF partner, based in western Orissa. Individual families decide to migrate depending on personal compulsions. In field interactions, families in Orissa admitted that they would not have to migrate if they could be certain that there would be two or three months' work available during the post monsoon lean period, it would provide them enough food security (this has implications for the National Rural Employment Guarantee Act). But most government work starts in the first half of the year, whereas the need of the migrant families is in the second half. Many mentioned that payment for government work done in the first half of the year comes several months late, and in the meanwhile they are forced to take advances from contractors. Several families said they migrated in the years when they needed cash for a marriage or a medical emergency or for death rites (this has implications for alternative credit mechanisms).

31. For example after the 2001 Gujarat earthquake, roof tiles factory owners of Morvi asked for tax exemptions.

NATURE OF WORK SITES

ALTHOUGH WORK SITES vary from sector to sector, there are certain elements that are common to most of them; they are usually far from habitation, in the wilderness with perhaps not even a road nearby. Consequently there are no basic facilities like water, a marketplace, a school or a health centre. Migrants depend on employers for their needs, which are not met to any degree of satisfaction. If there is habitation nearby, migrant labourers are usually shunned by local people, and regarded as bad elements or thieves. Locals erect extra fences around their homes to keep migrants out. They are subject to prejudice, and are stigmatised and criminalized. (Mosse 2005) There are no labour laws at the site. Work hours are long and odd, up to 16 hours daily and some sections of labourers have to be on call round the clock. Work norms are set keeping in mind healthy and strong young men, but everyone, including weaker, older men and women and children, has to struggle to meet them. A shortfall in performance means being weeded out of the labour force. Contractors retain control of labourers not only financially but also physically, forcing them to work even when they are sick or injured. Yet if employers stop or slow down the work for their own reasons, for example a technical snag in the production process, the payment also stops.

If working conditions are wretched living space is worse — tiny, unhygienic and inhuman. Most members of the family sleep under the open sky in all weather conditions. The nutrition available is sub-minimal. Health hazards are too numerous to list, and range from infections and fevers, contamination and toxicity related diseases, respiratory and gynaecological problems, injuries and accidents, malnourishment of children and so on. There are no facilities for medical treatment, and no compensations or insurance; on the contrary, if a worker falls ill and cannot work he gets no pay.

For women life on the site is worse than if they were living with the same marginalization in their homes in the village. Their work hours are longer as they have domestic and child rearing responsibilities in addition to working on the site. In the bargain, their nutrition, health, illnesses and need for rest take second place compared to the men. This gets carried down to the girls.

| HARD LABOUR, POOR PAY |

SUGARCANE SITES IN MAHARASHTRA

The settled sugarcane cutters (at the tyre and gadi centres[32]) camp for the season in clearings earmarked by factories for them in the vicinity of the fields. Each family is provided with a bamboo mat and poles, which are converted into a small conical hut or kopi (8 feet in diameter). Tyre centre settlements or 'addas' have 200-500 kopis and gadi centres have 50-100 kopis. The kopis are cramped together, and bullocks are parked in front of each. Animals and humans live together in congested conditions. The work units or koyatas move in the dark hours of the morning to fields where they cut cane throughout the day at the rate of 1.5 tonnes per person. The payment rate per tonne varies between Rs 80 and 100. The field is divided into strips, and each strip is assigned to one koyata for cutting — the man and woman cut the cane, remove the leaves, and throw it on the ground, the child takes the cane and puts it on a pile. The piles thus made are then tied into bundles, carried on the head by

Work sites are usually far from habitation, in the wilderness, with no basic facilities, not even a road nearby.

32. See FN pg 13.

At one field where cane cutting was going on, we observed seven koytas working simultaneously. Those who were faster had moved further into their 'strip' compared to others. As workers cut cane ceaselessly, the work site gave the uncanny appearance of being mechanized! There were about 15 adults at the site and about 13 children of all ages, the youngest being an infant tied in cloth hammock. The 4-6 year olds were around their parents, trying to work, constantly in danger of being hit by the sickle. The older children were fully part of the assembly line. When we tried to talk to some adults, after a few moments they moved back to work saying they had no time. When we tried to lift one of the bundles of cane we could not even budge it!

At sugarcane settlements animals and humans live together in congested conditions.

men and women and put on to carts.

The men drive the carts to the factory where they might have to wait in queue for several hours before they get to offload the cane. The women, meanwhile, walk several kilometres back to the settlement. In field interactions, many of them described how they fight exhaustion all the time.

The mobile sugarcane cutters (the doki centre koyatas) work in areas with less intensive cultivation and are, therefore, moved to new locations every 15-20 days by their agents. They do not have their own carts but are dependent on factory trucks. They also have no shelter and live in open, unprotected spaces and work in much smaller groups of 15-20, as compared with their tyre and gadi centre counterparts. Their output is tied to the factory schedule, which works round the clock. The koyatas are thus subjected to round the clock loading of trucks that ply up and down all day and night. Often they get to sleep only once in 2 or 3 days. Women and girls in doki centres are more exposed to exploitation.

The mobile sugarcane cutters have no shelter, they live in open unprotected spaces.

Jobs are assigned starting with the youngest children, according to their strength.

BRICK KILN SITES NEAR HYDERABAD

Although brick kilns can be seen scattered all over the countryside, their major concentration is found on peripheries of large urban centres, and these are the ones that attract large-scale migrant labour. A typical brick kiln may have 50-100 labourers including men, women and children. There are distinct processes within the brick kiln, which is set up like an assembly line. The work of a unit or pathuria, comprising a man, a woman and 2-3 children, involves mixing clay, making mud balls, moulding, carrying wet bricks to the field for drying, flipping them as they dry, carrying dried bricks as headloads to the kiln for firing and finally carrying headloads of ready bricks to trucks for transportation to the market. The pathuria is expected to make 1000 bricks per day for which it has to work continuously for 14-16 hours. For this a worker earns Rs 80 (divided by four this works out to Rs 20 per person per day). The contractor pays a family only 25-30 per cent of their earnings weekly for consumption.[33]

Jobs are 'assigned' starting from the youngest children. Four year olds have been observed sorting coal from a heap. "Children work according to their strength," as one parent at a Hyderabad kiln observed, pointing to a 4 year old girl carrying a brick, " after some time she will start carrying two!" Children of 9-11 years are fully part of the assembly line — they mix mud and straw, sieve coal dust, make balls of wet mud, carry wet bricks on the steel base plate to lay for drying, and flip them as they dry. A wet brick weighs 3 kilos. Once dried, they carry them in head loads of 10-12 bricks to the kiln. Many of these operations have been specifically designated to children due to their small hands and light bodies (like walking over semi dried bricks to flip them!) Moreover, parents believe that this work cannot proceed without children!

Families live next to the workspace in tiny, dingy, very low makeshift huts, which they erect out of broken bricks and some roofing material collected from the surroundings. In the Andhra Pradesh brick kiln areas, weekly markets come up for migrant labour, selling the poorest quality food (broken rice or chicken feed, dried or rotting vegetables and discarded portions of meat) at exorbitant prices.[34] The water for drinking is the same as that used for mixing clay for the bricks. This is what the families survive on for 8 months every year. Children aged 7-8 years look no more than 4 years old.

33. We were told their weekly wages are pegged below the train fare back to their homes, so that they do not run away.

34. Broken rice or chicken feed which sells at Rs 3-4 per Kg in the market sells here for Rs 7-8 per Kg.

Children not only work for as many hours as their parents, they also suffer the same verbal and physical abuse. Terrible scenes have been witnessed, specially in AP kilns, like the instance of a girl who was trying to make her younger brother, shivering with fever, get up because she was unable to carry all the bricks to the kiln, under threat of the supervisor. They suffer from respiratory, stomach, eye and skin problems along with water-related diseases; many children become knock-kneed. Accidents due to burns are also common, which cause disability and even death, but are completely ignored by employers. The girls and women are constantly exposed to sexual abuse.

SALTPANS IN GUJARAT

The saltpans or agars provide by far the harshest natural conditions to live and work in. Marine saltpans are located on, or a little inland from, the coastline. A typical agar is spread over a 10-acre area, and is serviced by the one family of two adults and 2-4 children that lives there. Their job is to make the saline seawater into a concentrate, exposed as it is to the sunlight, by circulating it over large areas from one pan to another, till it finally crystallizes into salt. The workers face harsh natural conditions at the pans, day after day — strong sea winds, the glare of the sun reflecting off the salt, strong mid-day heat and chilly night temperatures. The working implements are heavy and ill designed and workers have hardly any protective devices like boots or gloves as they work, wading in the brine all day long. According to prescribed rules and regulations the government and employers are supposed to provide salt workers with housing, water, transport, fuel, and medical, educational and other facilities, but none of this is available.

Infants and babies grow up in such disorganized conditions that their development is affected.

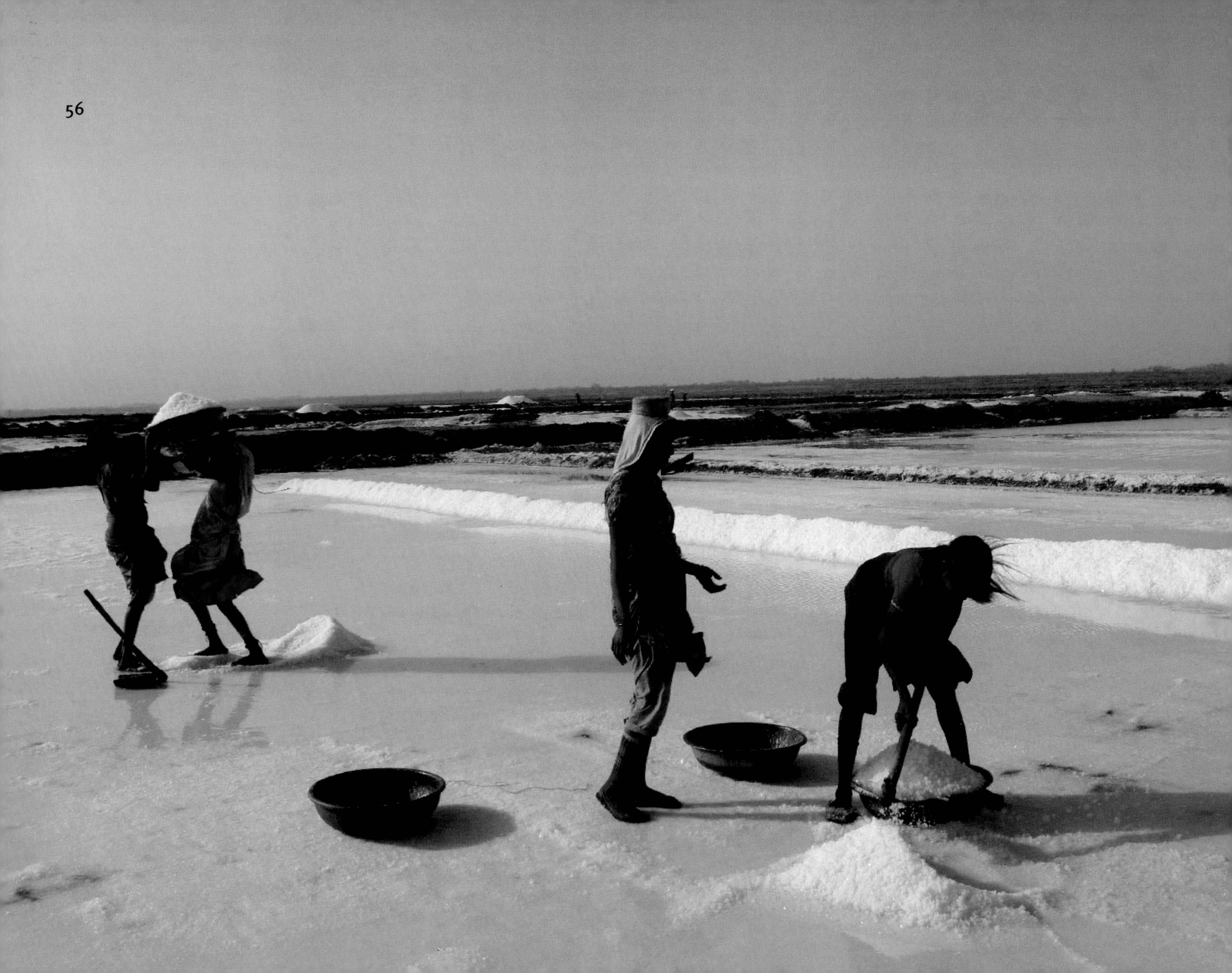

At a saltpan in Saurashtra we met a girl who was about 10 years old. She said her mother and father worked through the night at the pan to avoid the midday heat, while she and her two younger siblings slept alone in the tiny hut quite some distance away. Every morning she woke up at 4:00 to cook food, which she did more or less in the darkness, never having enough supply of kerosene to light the lamp. Then she walked about a kilometre and a half with the food to the saltpan to give it to her parents. She came back to collect water and fire wood, following which she washed clothes and then fed her two siblings. She remained busy till her parents returned by 10 am to sleep for a few hours. After this the parents again went back to the pan. This time she and the other two children accompanied them to the pan, to lend a hand there till evening. This was the routine she had been following everyday since the time they migrated about six months back. She told us she accompanied her parents each year.

The family lives in a shack made of wood and plastic sheets, which is open to wind and cold. Supply of water and food is uncertain and meagre. A person has to go to the nearest town for supplies once every two weeks, bringing back the limited amount he can carry on a bicycle or on foot.

To avoid the peak afternoon sun, salt workers cut into their nighttime, toiling in complete darkness, alone, on the vast pans. Children have no specific activities, but assist their parents in all the tasks, all day long. Girls take the responsibility of collecting firewood, cooking and carrying food to the saltpan.

Salt workers face the additional deprivation of social isolation. A family of 4-5 lives a lonesome existence on their pan with the next pan and its workers several kilometres away.

Payments are made per tonne of salt produced. A work unit takes an advance of Rs 2,000-5,000 and has an average monthly income of Rs 1,000 (for 8 months). After deduction of advances, consumption, and so on, a family may take back on an average not more that Rs 3,000-4,000 at the end of the season. But many families remain perpetually in debt to the contractor.

Salt workers face harsh natural conditions at the pans, day after day.

WOMEN AND GIRLS AT WORK SITES

The gender aspect of distress migrations needs to be specially addressed. Women fighting on two fronts — labour and home

— get far less rest than men. Domestic violence erupts easily. Pregnant women also have no respite. Poor nutritionand lack of medical help leads to unwanted abortions. Lactating mothers hardly get feeding breaks.

Sexual exploitation is another reality of migrations. Women and adolescent girls are frequently exposed to sexual abuse, especially at the hands of contractors and truck drivers. They travel on trucks and trains amidst men at all odd hours. The fear and insecurity of having to sleep in the open, many say, has taught them to sleep intermittently. They have to also defecate and bathe in the open. In Jhabua district of Madhya Pradesh, the town of Alirajpur in a high migration block reportedly registers a high rate of abortions when labourers return from migration.[35] HIV/AIDS is fast taking root among migrants, and the National Aids Control Organisation is focusing its interventions in this sector.

CHILD LABOUR AT WORK SITES

Due to the nature of wage payment based on piece rate, children from a young age get drawn into labour by contractors and parents. Thus while children are not 'employed' and no employer ever acknowledges child labour at work sites, they benefit nevertheless from the 'subsidy' of this free labour, which is significant in volume but gets subsumed as 'family labour'.[36] In almost every sector, sets of tasks are delineated for children. In the brick kilns children are an integral part of the assembly line. Girls stay back in the settlements and manage household chores, giving their parents more time to work. Minding younger siblings is one of the major responsibilities of older girls and many parents take their older daughters along for this purpose.

Children have minimal access to clean drinking water, nutri-tion, proper clothing or hygienic conditions. The ruthless environment of the work sites deprives them of the minimum care, support or love. Not only are they abused by contractors, but also face the wrath of exhausted parents, including mothers who have no respite from hardship themselves. Children are exposed to all sorts of insecurities and hazards at work sites, from burns to cuts and snakebites. When sick they get no treatment. Even in case of major illnesses, parents are helpless and cannot get proper treatment.

Infants and babies face terrible neglect, as their parents toil away. They just cry most of the time, as one field worker described. They grow up in such disorganized conditions that their development is affected. And from the moment they get on their feet they start getting into work. Parents, for want of back-up support, also bring children with physical and mental disabilities along, and often leave them alone at the settlements all day long while they go to work.[37]

NGOs encounter a great deal of resistance from employers to opening schools or pre-primary centres at work sites. But with their persistent efforts hundreds of 'hidden' children have become visible, which is itself silent and powerful advocacy.

The common feature of all types of migration sites is that over the last several decades no improvement is reported in the working and living conditions of the labourers, while employers and industry continue to rake in huge profits. Technological change, in terms of improved tools and implements, has also bypassed the workers in these sectors.

At a brick kiln site, we met a woman who had been beaten and turned out by her husband because she objected to his relations with another woman. She had found her way to this other brick kiln where a family from her village worked. We found her sitting with her small bundle of possessions, but this family could do little but show indifference to her.

35. In informal conversations with district officials of Sarva Shiksha Abhiyan, Madhya Pradesh.
36. In conversation with Prof Jean Dreze.
37. Janarth's baseline of 2005-06 has shown 96 children with different types of disabilities at the work sites.

Children have minimal access to clean drinking water, nutrition, proper clothing or hygienic conditions.

IMPACT ON THE LIVES OF MIGRANTS

Migrants lead an uprooted life belonging neither to their villages nor to the places where they go.

ALTHOUGH seasonal migration is becoming a major annual occurrence in many parts of rural and, more specifically, tribal India, not enough is known about its impact on the personal lives of migrants and the social fabric of the villages they leave behind. Some things, however, have become clear from research studies and field visits and these are discussed below.

| DYING COMMUNITIES, DYING VILLAGES |

Being away from home and village, migrants lead an uprooted life. They do not belong to the places where they go, and increasingly lose acceptance in their own villages. Cut off from their community, culture and traditions, unable to take part in festivals, fairs and religious and social functions, which are an important part of their lives, migrants lose their sense of identity. The vulnerability of people who cross state boundaries is even greater as they are unfamiliar with the language and culture of the areas they go to and they find themselves increasingly at the mercy of their contractors.

While migrating families face hardships, the elderly, ailing family members or children left behind in villages have difficulty fending for themselves, and are often reduced to destitution. They frequently do not know where the family has gone, or how to contact them. Dealing with emergencies, particularly back home is difficult, especially for those who go long distance. They have to spend money on travel, and forego earnings for the days they are away. News of injury or death takes a considerable amount of time to reach. For instance, recently in the Setu field area 12 saltpan migrants died in a bus accident, and their co-workers had no way of contacting their families. There are reports of people going missing, or women being carried off, and people at home are helpless to do anything. Further, poor and unhealthy working conditions ensure that most migrants rapidly decline into ill health. It is said of Orissa brick migrants that after four or five years in the brick kilns a young man starts to look old and haggard.

Another subject that needs careful study is how this annual phenomenon of seasonal migration impacts the social set up of villages. The effect differs in villages with mixed populations, as compared with those that have a predominantly SC/ST population. In mixed villages as the population of the lower strata moves out for extended periods each year, their interactions with the upper strata reduce greatly. Even links with their own community members in the village weaken. Their representation in village institutions reduces. As their voice gets diminished, little attention is given to their needs and demands. Because of their reduced/erratic presence in the village migrants are not taken seriously in any quarter, with villagers having the attitude that 'they will soon be leaving'.

In villages that have a largely SC/ST population, migration levels may go up to 70-80 per cent or even 100 per cent in some cases. Such villages remain more or less empty for much of the year, with just a few elderly people in some homes. The effect on the social set up of the village can be imagined — no one to celebrate festivals, or observe religious mores, or maintain village assets; hardly any panchayat activity, and the local health centre and school in a state of disuse. These are initial but critical

field observations that underline the need for further research if we are to understand the full impact of this.

| INCREASING ASSETLESSNESS |

Distress migrants find themselves on a relentless falling curve as far as assets go. They start by being landless or land poor, with hardly any skills, assets or education. Earnings from migration are survival level and allow them no opportunity to build assets. On the contrary, medical or other personal emergencies as well as the unstable nature of work often push them further into debt. Their meagre possessions are also at perpetual risk. Families who lock their homes and leave find their dwellings and other possessions in a state of disrepair or disuse when they return. Those who own a few animals have to arrange that they are cared for in the village and they have to pay for this. Many just end up selling them off at low prices. The work at the sites allows for no advancement or upward mobility. The few who have the advantage of some education experience frustration at being unable to get out of the trap. Clearly education is a necessary but not sufficient condition to enable assetless migrants to get out of the traps within which they are caught. Eventually, the last asset of the migrant is the body, which is used as collateral to get an advance from the contactor. But years of migration and extreme physical abuse wear out their bodies way ahead of their years — contractors find diminishing use for labourers who are beyond 40 years of age.

| CITIZENS WITHOUT RIGHTS |

Documents such as PDS (Public Distribution System) or BPL (Below Poverty Line) cards and caste certificates lose relevance

for migrants where they go. Orissa tribals mortgage their BPL cards for a meagre sum, and usually cannot retrieve them on return. They have to forego free health services and schooling facilities for their children in their villages. Their infants do not get covered in the immunization drives. They lose the opportunity to participate in panchayat activities. They cannot benefit from government schemes or NGO initiatives like self-help groups, literacy classes, etc. They are not eligible for micro credit interventions of NGOs, because they are not present in villages to make weekly or monthly repayments.

As the migrant population moves out for extended periods each year their links in their villages weaken.

*Migrant children
face a life of
hardship and
rootlessness right
from infancy.*

At their destination points migrants are outside the system and cannot avail of what they are foregoing in their villages. They have to buy grain, kerosene and other basic commodities at market prices. As work sites are away from habitation, there are no government health centres or schools nearby, nor are migrants eligible to make use of them. Claiming entitlements is difficult for household members left behind in the village. Migrants cannot vote in elections that usually take place during the migration months. Interestingly, local politicians ensure the votes of short distance migrants in panchayat elections, by having them brought over in trucks. However, seasonal migrants are often not included in the census, as this usually takes place during the first half of the year which coincides with the migration period. In the coastal areas of Gujarat, which are frequently struck by cyclones, labourers working on marine saltpans get washed away, and there is no record of people who have died in this way. Migrant fisherfolk in the same region may inadvertently cross the border and find themselves in Pakistani territory, ending up in jails. Some local NGOs are aware of these ocurrences and try to bring them to light. The migrant takes all this in his stride in his quest for survival.

All policy and planning in this country is geared towards the 'fixed' residence: the village, the block, the district, the state. Migration however, defies this: large sections of population that happen to be the most vulnerable, live with frequent changes of location and unpredictable patterns of movement which have become a way of life. Not that this phenomenon is restricted to the poor and the marginalized — the upper strata of society also does migrate and change locations — but their rights and entitlements move with them. The lowest strata leave their rights and entitle-

ments behind, becoming thoroughly disenfranchised. These are equal citizens of the country, but disempowered in every possible respect — social, economic, educational and even political (they are nobody's vote bank) — and have nothing to fall back on but

DECLARATION OF THE RIGHTS OF THE CHILD

Principle 2: The child... shall be given opportunities and facilities, by law and by other means, to enable him to develop physically, mentally, morally, spiritually and socially in a healthy and normal manner and in conditions of freedom and dignity.

Principle 4: ...The child shall have the right to adequate nutrition, housing, recreation and medical services.

Principle 7: The child is entitled to receive education, which shall be free and compulsory, at least in the elementary stages. The child shall have full opportunity for play and recreation

Principle 9: The child shall be protected against all forms of neglect, cruelty and exploitation... The child shall not be admitted to employment before an appropriate minimum age; he shall in no case be caused or permitted to engage in any occupation or employment which would prejudice his health or education, or interfere with his physical, mental or moral development.

their bodies, their manual labour. The irony is that this most disadvantaged group and informal sector, the migrants — in their massive numbers, and their huge and diverse outputs seen in aggregation — generate 'super profits' for the employers and industries that thrive on the 'subsidy' of their labour.

| CHILDREN - BORN TO UPROOTED LIVES? |

Migrant children face a life of hardship and rootlessness right from infancy. Many are born at work sites, to overworked, undernourished mothers, in dingy, unhygienic dwellings with zero medical assistance. The mother is forced back to work soon after childbirth, and has no opportunity to rest or to care for her infant. Babies are left by themselves or in the care of an older sibling. A distressing lack of nutrition, mother's care, hygiene, medical assistance, basic comfort and security characterize the life of the baby migrant at a work site. Babies and toddlers use their parents work implements as playthings. Crawling close to furnaces, cutting themselves on sickles, getting bitten by insects are everyday occurrences for these children. Their illnesses remain untreated. They receive no immunization. The list is endless... and all this happens despite India being a signatory to the UN Child Rights Charter.

As children grow older and are subjected to hazardous travel between villages and work sites year after year, they start working "according to their strength", and as we have seen earlier, parents believe that children have the strength to lift and carry things even at age four! Although this fact is never acknowledged, even by parents, careful observation at all types of work sites reveals how even the youngest children start getting involved in specific tasks, like sifting coal dust, collecting and

bundling sugarcane tops, carrying bricks, etc., and how through these they are 'apprenticed' into adult tasks. The very presence of children at work sites makes it inevitable that they rapidly get sucked into hard labour. By the age of 11-12 they become full-fledged labourers.

In the village, even if the children get enrolled in schools, they find no acceptance there, and are constantly viewed as outsiders by teachers and children alike. Their school attendance is hardly for four months, from July to October. Now most children's names are on the school rolls due to recent enrolment drives. School authorities are complacent in this knowledge and do not keep track of the large numbers who leave school around November, and stay out until the end of the academic session; their names remain on the registers. Attendance plummets, but regis-

ters often do not reflect this. Those responsible for monitoring schools also do not highlight this issue. On their return, schools make it difficult for migrant children to get reintegrated — because of the requirement of attendance and exam records. Children end up repeating the class and the lack of support from teachers and administration leads to a large number of drop outs.

Government surveys for out-of-school children are targeted at villages, and take place usually during the migration period. Thus hundreds of thousands of children who have left for migration sites are never counted. Undernourished, uncared for, uneducated, voiceless, invisible and violated, children of migrant labour are condemned to a life that shames the Constitution of this country and all the legislation that is in place to protect them and ensure a positive, hope-filled future.

| WOMEN AND GIRLS — CAN ANYONE SUFFER MORE? |

The gender dimension of distress migrations needs to be specially investigated. There are three aspects to this: The first is to do with the arduous labour that women have to perform, which is considerably beyond the capacities of their emaciated bodies. The second is to do with male violence, from which women have no respite whatever their circumstances. The causes for this are the usual ones — extra demands from men on the home front, drinking, sexual relations outside marriage, etc. But the vulnerability of women to deal with these issues is far greater given their precarious life condition at work sites; The third is to do with the female body. Physical and sexual abuse of women and girls by contractors, agents and others is a hard reality of migrations.

STATE RESPONSES

LOCAL AND LARGER state machineries tend to overlook their migrant population — this is in evidence in every state and sector, and is equally true of the bureaucratic, the political as well as the legislative set up. Even the media have failed to address this crucial issue. Further, as we have seen, schools, too, are not sympathetic to migrant children, closing the only opportunity for the younger generation to break out of this cycle. Below, we take a brief look at the role of the state with respect to the migrant population:

BUREAUCRATIC IGNORANCE OR NEGLECT?

The scale of seasonal migration is large, running into hundreds of thousands in many states, but unrecorded and mostly invisible. Most migration sectors fall within the unorganized sector, which constitutes 93 per cent of the labour force of India. The majority of migration work sites are found to be unregulated; therefore there is neither data available on the magnitude and nature of work force employed there, nor a check on the working and living conditions of migrants. In the brick industry for example, thousands of kilns are unregistered and exist illegally. Field experience in Gujarat and Andhra Pradesh testifies to this, and this is likely to be the case in brick kilns all over the country.

In the sending areas, the labour department at district and state levels has no authentic record of migrant labour — their numbers, the type of work they migrate for, the destinations they go to, their periods of absence, etc. Bolangir district of Orissa sends out 100,000-150,000 labourers every year, but the labour office records show just a few hundred.

Due to this under-enumeration of seasonal migrants policy planners are not adequately aware of the extent and nature of the phenomenon, and as a result the required attention to address this issue and frame specific policies for the alleviation of distress is lacking. The state has pathetically failed to preserve the traditional livelihoods of, or provide alternative livelihoods to, large sections of its citizens, and as these impoverished, marginalized families tear themselves away from their homes, communities and villages to look for subsistence income, the state just turns away. As already described, state welfare measures are not geared to serve the needs and circumstances of seasonal migrants. While the country will ensure that even the soldiers posted at Siachen glacier caste their vote, tens of millions of migrant families, living all around the country, have no means to do the same. The migrants do not feature in the Five Year Plans. There are no special schemes for their benefit. Ironically, while tribal areas specifically witness the heaviest outmigration, the Tribal Area Development Programmes (TAD) have no components that address the issue of migration.

The refusal by state governments to acknowledge seasonal migration into or out of their states has allowed a nexus of corruption and malpractices to grow: budgetary and other allocations are made to districts and blocks according to population size, but as large sections of the population move out every year for several months, the funds, the PDS and midday meal (MDM) grains, and so on, remain unaccounted for and go to line various pockets. Primary health centres (PHCs), schools and other services are content to work at a reduced load.

Programmes such as Lok Jumbish in Rajasthan and the District Primary Education Program (DPEP) did recognize in small ways that

The local ActionAid office in Bolangir district of Orissa discovered that the railway station of Kantabhanji, the hub where migrants are collected from and transported to AP, used to proudly display a chart of monthly train reservations. In two weeks of November in a recent year, the graph shot up from a few hundred to 40,000! ActionAid people had to take recourse to that graph to prove their point to the local officials. Not surprisingly, the graph was withdrawn from public display after that.

children were being left out of education due to seasonal migration. Small efforts were made to cover a few villages and work sites, and it was then that the idea of seasonal hostel and site schools originated. But these programmes ended after a while. Yet the EGS and AIE scheme formulated under the DPEP, and carried forward under SSA, does recognize migrant children as a category of out-of-school children. Some state governments have, however, begun to take note of the issue. In Andhra Pradesh and Orissa officials have initiated discussions about the rights and entitlements of migrant labour and the education of their children. The Madhya Pradesh government has taken the step of starting seasonal hostels in over 700 villages in 40 districts in 2005, where migrant children can go to school while their parents migrate. In the past, Gujarat's education department also started an initiative of tracking migrant children through school. Recently, the government of Maharashtra also decided to start seasonal hostels in all sending areas of the state. Since 2005-06 the SSA has been pushing, at the central level, the agenda of assessing the scale of migration with the states and planning for their coverage. The process of introducing this as a mandatory requirement in the SSA framework has begun. These are small beginnings. But the scale of the problem is mammoth, and growing. The central government needs to take full responsibility towards these disenfranchised citizens.

Recently, the draft Unorganised Sector Workers' Social Security Bill 2006, took note of seasonal migrants. Related issues such as universal registration, a social security package (covering risk due to illness, death, permanent stoppage of earnings), self-declaration of domicile and the possibility of extending the benefits of other public programmes to them in locations outside their homes are under discussion.

Children seem to be the most unprotected despite a gamut of protective legislation.

The scale of distress seasonal migration appears to be mammoth, and growing.

| INEFFECTIVE LEGISLATION |

Interestingly, there is substantial legislation in place to protect the rights of labour, including children. The following are Acts that would have a direct or indirect bearing on different aspects of migration:

> Interstate Migrant Workmen Act (1979);
> Contract Labour System (Regulation and Abolition) Act (1970);
> The Child Labour (Prohibition and Regulation) Act (1986);
> The Bonded Labour System (Abolition) Act (1975);
> The Minimum Wages Act (1948);
> The Equal Remuneration Act (1976) for Women;
> The Construction Workers Act (1996);
> The Factories Act (1948);
> The Trade Union Act (1926).

However, when it comes to comprehensively covering migrant workers, there are serious inadequacies in the legislation. The lacunae in implementation of existing legislation are also enormous. This renders the migrant worker more or less unprotected, with no grievance redress mechanism, and thoroughly exploited. The Interstate Migrant Workmen Act (1979), the primary legal instrument to regulate migration is also ridden with numerous problems. To begin with, it applies only to those migrants who go through a contractor. But contractors and officials project that people are migrating on their own without the aid of a contractor to escape enforcement of this law. Secondly, the Act requires that contractors register themselves with the Labour Office and get licenses. But hardly any contractor has a licence. According to the provisions of this Act the migration sites should be registered, for example, brick kilns should be registered under the Factories Act. This however is rarely the case, and employers not only evade all norms openly, but also escape prosecution if ever the occasion arises.

The Interstate Migrant Workmen Act does not satisfactorily address the issue of child labour, and leaves a great deal to interpretation. One such interpretation is that children accompanying their parents cannot be called child labourers. When it comes to children's wages, the Child Labour Act, 1986, does not deal with the issue. For this one has to go to the Minimum Wages Act. Child labour is rampant in all migration sectors, especially in the Orissa brick migrations; it is well known that the child is an essential part of the work unit. Besides, there are many sectors which exclusively employ migrant child labour. As employers realize that child labour is the cheapest labour that can be accessed, and offers the least resistance, the trend of segmenting the work is increasing, and more and more processes are being found for children to perform. In the end, children seem to be the most unprotected despite this entire gamut of legislation.

NGOs and grassroots activists have expressed a strong need for revision of the interstate Migrant Workmen Act. Such a revision is also necessary in light of the fact that over the last 25 years seasonal migration has undergone a sea change, its scale and scope has changed beyond recognition, and it is continuing to grow. Appropriate legislation needs to be framed for migrant workers in today's context. Furthermore, the Act only addresses interstate migration, and today substantial migration is taking place within the state. A demand has been voiced for states to formulate legislation related to intrastate migration as well.

SECTION II
interventions in education

THE INTERVENTIONS

| THE CONTEXT AND APPROACH |

SEASONAL MIGRATION is a highly complex phenomenon. While planning interventions that address its causes and consequences, it is necessary to take into account a range of factors like the vast areas over which the migration is spread, the distances between sending and receiving ends, the nature of work sites, the pattern of mobility of the migrant community, the instability and lack of autonomy in their lives, the issues related to employers and labour agents, the unpredictability of the migratory seasons and, in the case of interstate migration the need to interact with more than one state administration, and so on.

It is also significant to note that in areas where seasonal migration occurs on scale there are hardly any NGOs working on education or migration. NGOs in such areas are found to be working mostly on livelihoods, and while their work indirectly mitigates distress mobility, there are not many that address the phenomenon of migration directly. The four NGOs whose work forms the content of this section were also new to these issues when they started the work three or four years ago. AIF played the role of engaging with them on issues of education and migration, and building their capacities.

This study was commissioned by AIF and the case studies of four of its partners lead to insights that could be valuable elsewhere. The fact that these case studies are located in different geographical and climatic regions brings a wider perspective to this work. The four NGOs are:

> Janarth in Aurangabad, Maharashtra, which began work on sugarcane migrations in Maharashtra in 2002.

> Setu in Ahemdabad, Gujarat, which began work with saltpan, brick kiln, charcoal and roof tile migrations in Gujarat in 2004.
> Vikalpa, located in western Orissa which began work on brick kiln migrations to Andhra Pradesh in 2004.
> Lok Drishti, located in western Orissa which began work on brick kiln migrations to Andhra Pradesh in 2004.

| THE OBJECTIVES |

The broad objectives of the four programmes are in line with the Sarva Shiksha Abhiyan, as defined below:

> No child of 0-14 years at work sites
> Access to school, participation and quality learning for every child
> Every child to complete the elementary education cycle

All four programmes aim to build models for quality interventions in education over a range of migration sectors and geographies. These are models that are in line with the Sarva Shiksha Abhiyan (SSA) framework and can therefore be taken to scale by the government of the state in question at a later stage, and can also ensure continuity of schooling for children through the elementary cycle.

| PROGRAMME INTERVENTIONS |

The four programme interventions were made by four different NGOs. As already mentioned, while these NGOs were new to education and were focusing on the migrant population for the first time, they had strong community linkages and an empowerment based approach to their work. This helped them a great deal in picking up the technicalities of the new work quickly. The four programme interventions are described briefly below:

Planning education interventions for children of seasonal migrants requires a range of factors to be taken into account.

| THE JANARTH EXPERIENCE |

The Marathwada region of central Maharashtra is highly arid, and four or five of its districts send migrant labour to the seven western water-rich sugar districts. As mentioned before, 650,000 labourers migrate every year for sugarcane harvesting, of which 200,000 are children. The state has 186 sugar factories,[40] of which, on an average, 100 become operational every year. Each factory receives 4000-6000 migrants who work in a 25-60 kilometre radius around the factory. Those who work in the inner ten kilometre radius live in settlements of 100-500 families. Several such settlements may be dotted in the hinterland of each factory. Those further away have less supply of cane, so they cannot settle but remain mobile and move, in groups of 8-10 families, from site to site looking for cane. The former are called 'tyre centres' and 'gadi centres' and the latter 'doki centres'.[41] It is easier to plan education interventions for the settled migrants, but far more difficult for the mobile ones.

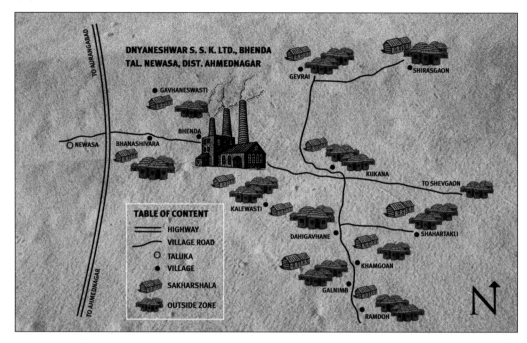

SAKHARSHALAS — SCHOOLS FOR MIGRANT CHILDREN AT SUGARCANE SITES

Janarth is running the Sakharshala Programme[42] spread over seven districts covering around 12,000 children of sugarcane cutters. Sakharshalas[43] are alternate schools for children of migrant labour and are run at work sites. Their purpose is to achieve universal coverage at these sites. The initiative began as a pilot project in 2002 in two factories covering around 600 children. Since then the programme has evolved and many new dimensions have been added to it. Currently, Janarth runs 142 sakharshalas in 35 factories, reaching out to nearly one-third of the total operational factories.

Sakharshalas are short term schools set up at labourers' settlements or addas for six months of the migration period. They run in temporary structures made of bamboo mats and metal pipes. Each school has 75-100 children. There is one classroom and one teacher for every 25 children. Each sakharshala has a pre-primary centre attached to it that caters to children of the 3-5 year age group. In 2003, the first year of the programme, only the primary age group (6-11 years) was covered, but from the second year onwards classes were started for the upper primary

LAYOUT OF SITES AROUND A SUGAR FACTORY

40. Of these 96 factories are located in western Maharashtra.
41. A survey by Janarth reveals that two-thirds of the migrant labour works at the tyre centres and one-third at the doki and gadi centres.
42. With 50 per cent financial support from Banyan Tree Foundation (BTF).
43. A Marathi coined term, means 'sugar school'.

Sakharshalas are schools run at work sites for children of sugarcane migrants.

Janarth is running the Sakharshala Programme spread over seven districts covering around 12,000 children.

82

age group (11-14 years) as well. By this age children are more entrenched into labour, and it is difficult to convince parents to relieve them from work; in the project areas the sakharshalas have gradually begun to attract older children as well. Now they cater to the 3-14 year age group. There is a conscious focus on getting girls to school. This is reflected in a good gender balance in sakharshalas with 46 per cent of the children being girls. A survey of the children with disabilities is also done every year at the work sites. Parents who have no support in the village also bring along children with physical and mental disabilities, although this number is very small.

Sakharshalas follow the government syllabus. The attendance and examination records of children are sent to their respective village schools, on the basis of which they can seek readmission on their return. Janarth is working to improve learning outcomes by introducing pedagogy suitable to the needs of migrant children. Teacher recruitment for sakharshalas is a big challenge, because the work sites are in remote areas with hardly any facilities. Also since these schools run only for about six months, teachers do not get paid for the rest of the year. Janarth has been trying to deal with the high turnover of teachers, by hiring more people from the sending areas, who can be absorbed in the villages after migration is over. Twenty five per cent of the teachers are women, which is an achievement for Janarth. All pre-primary centre caretakers are women, and they are selected from among the migrants. Initially Janarth's coverage was limited to the settled migrants, who constitute not more than 40-50 per cent of the total labour received by a factory. But now Janarth is finding ways to cover mobile migrants also, through 'shifting

schools' and other strategies. Janarth aims to eventually create a model of complete coverage of a factory.

SEASONAL HOSTELS IN VILLAGES

The original assumption of this programme was that during the migration period children would attend sakharshalas, and on their return, go back to the village schools. Follow up, however, was difficult. Data revealed that the children came from around 400 villages spread over four to five districts. Further, the next season saw new faces in the sakharshalas. Since families driven by agents do not necessarily come back to the same factory every year, maintaining the continuity of the children's education is a challenge. In the course of Janarth's work, two things have become clear — one, that eventually there must be schools at all migration sites — a task that only the state is capable of doing; two, there is need to work in the villages also. Unless education is captured at both the sending and the receiving ends, the efforts made so far will not bear fruit, and the initiative will remain short lived.

In 2004 Janarth conducted a study of 165 sending villages in 53 high migration blocks of four districts.[44] Among other things, the study threw light on issues to do with local schools: their reluctance to readmit migrant children, promote them to the next class, give them additional support in their studies, and so on. While the excuses given were non-learning, and a lack of attendance and examination records, teachers were not free of biases against these children. Migrant children, therefore, dropped out or stagnated in one grade year after year, something that calls for dialogue at community, school and state level.

44. Beed, Jalgaon, Ahmadnagar & Jalna

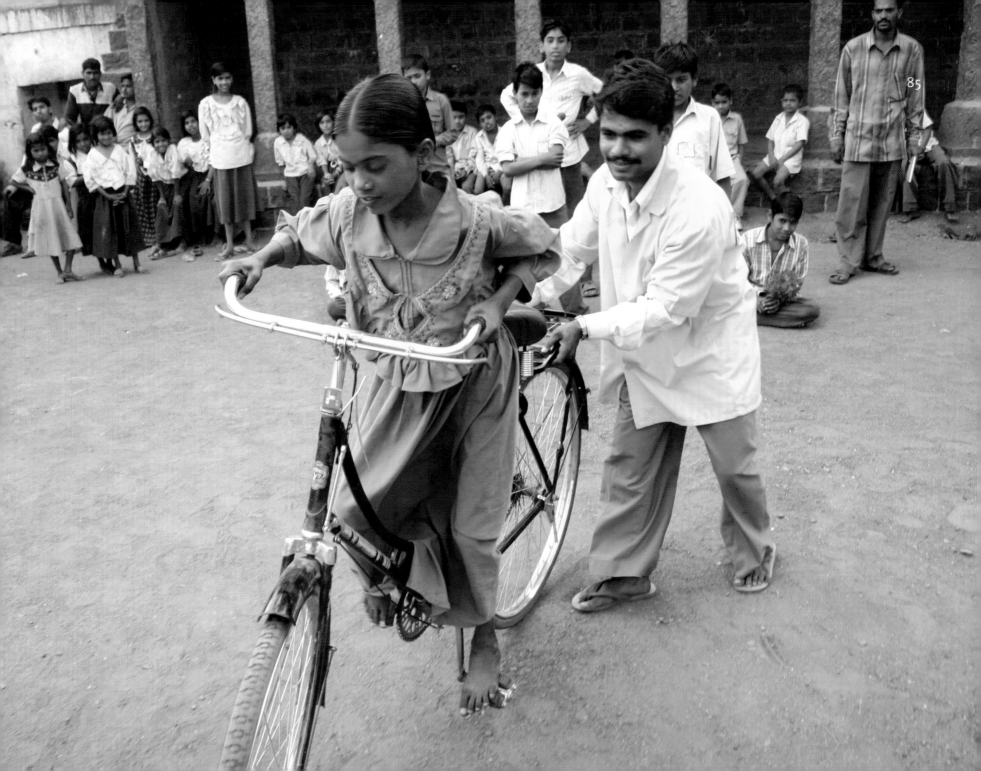

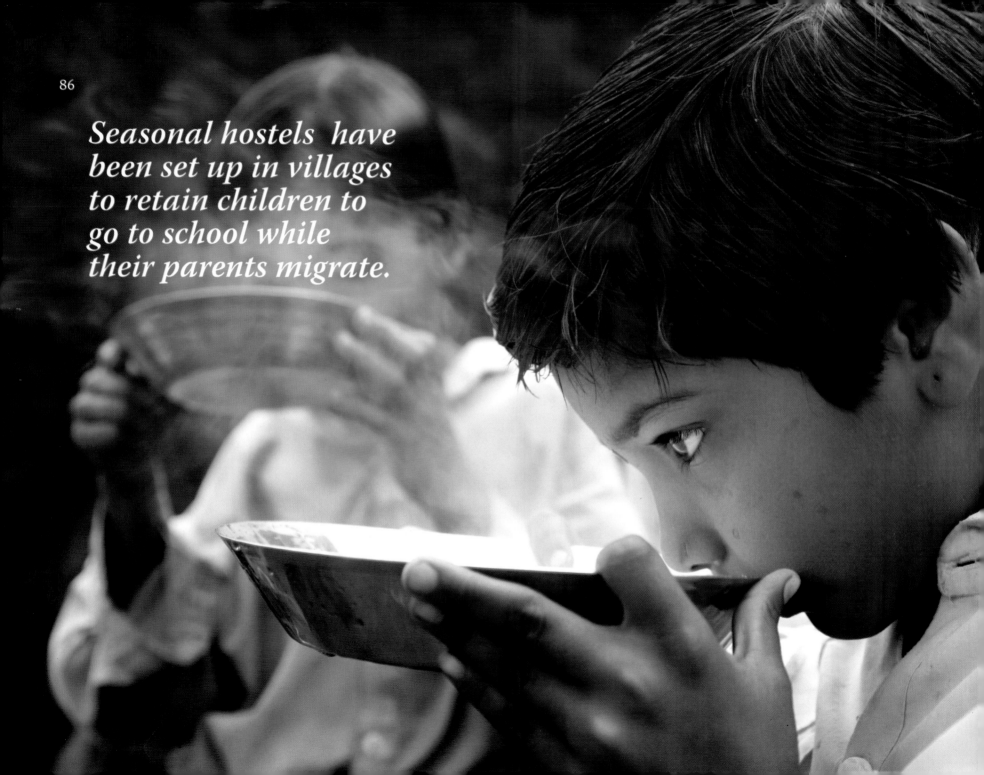

Seasonal hostels have been set up in villages to retain children to go to school while their parents migrate.

CASE STUDY 1

It also became evident that parents who migrate have a strong desire to send their children to school, and those who can afford to do so try and leave at least one or two children behind with relatives in the villages.[45] But not all parents are able to do so. In order to systematize the education of children, the creation of seasonal hostels[46] in the village came up as a demand from the community, specially the weaker sections which have no backup support.

From 2005 onwards Janarth has extended its operations in the sending areas by starting seasonal hostels in nine villages in two blocks[47] of Beed district. The hostels, which were run in community halls or homes of migrants, retained 450 migrant children from grades I to VII, of whom 36 per cent were girls. Each hostel had 30 children, one caretaker and one cook. Separate spaces were organized in the hostel premises for girls and boys to sleep, bathe and so on. As expected, parents were initially apprehensive about leaving their children behind, especially as in Maharashtra, people migrate across long distances and coming back is usually not possible. But when the migrants got news of the hostels doing well, some of the families organized for one person to take their children back to the village and leave them in the hostel. Interestingly, Janarth's initiative served as inspiration for the CEO of the adjoining Ahmadnagar district to take over 21 hostels which Janarth was preparing to start, and run them with district funds. The standards maintained by Janarth hostels worked as a benchmark for the government hostels.

The hostels received a great deal of support from the village residents (non-migrant community). They became a hub for all children in the village, many of whom started joining up for morn-

45. The CDRD study also shows that the average family size at the factory is 3.5 of which two are adults and the rest are children.
46. A seasonal hostel is a facility to prevent migration of children, and keep them back in the village in the care of hostel staff, teachers and community. These hostels run for the 6-8 months of the migration period and disband once the parents come back.
47. Ashti and Shirur.

ing exercises and evening games and classes. Each hostel has a bicycle and all the children, specially the girls, proudly claim that they have learnt to ride it. Elders also regularly come to watch and participate. At the end of the season, demands started to come from many adjoining villages for a similar facility.

Janarth is encouraged by its initial success, and is working to build on many areas. The main one is to do with girls — while the gender balance achieved in the first year is commendable in a residential programme, systems have to be strengthened so that girls can freely participate in all activities. The other is to do with overall security and safety of the children. Together with this there is also a plan to run bridge courses in the summer months for those children who could neither stay back in the seasonal hostels, nor get enrolled in sakharshalas. Through these multiple options — seasonal hostel, sakharshalas and bridge courses — it is hoped that the every child will get covered and the programme will move towards universal coverage of migrant children in project villages and work sites.

STRENGTHENING LOCAL VILLAGE SCHOOLS

The third important dimension of the programme is to address the local school. Apart from the issues of migrant children, Janarth's study showed that the functioning of schools in general was quite unsatisfactory. There was a shortage of teachers and of textbooks, non-accountability, low performance, lack of supervision, and over and above this, very low learning outcomes. Consequently, many non-migrant children were also dropping out of schools. Clearly, unless the school and educational facilities improved, all efforts towards retaining migrant children would go waste. Thus Janarth

has undertaken to strengthen the local schools and ensure coverage and retention of all children in the village including non-migrants. This is being done through enlisting community support, and engaging with block and district officials to ensure proper provisioning and functioning in schools.

The experiences of the first year have been encouraging. The presence of the hostel in the village has given a boost to the school. Now the school, which used to be neglected before, is the focus of the whole village. As the hostel children maintain a proper routine, and come to school on time, others have also

started to do so. Attendance and punctuality have gone up. Not only are teachers now more regular, some of them also show greater enthusiasm to teach. The community is now beginning to look critically at the school and its functioning. As hostel children do their homework regularly in evening classes, many village children also join them in doing so — this began when residents requested that these classes be open to all children. These are just some of the initial changes, seen in all nine villages. With systematic work in the coming years Janarth hopes to help schools improve further, in a number of aspects.

ADVOCACY WITH FACTORY MANAGEMENTS

In the beginning Janarth faced strong resistance from factory managements for setting up the sakharshalas. Some factories refused to acknowledge the presence of children at sugarcane sites. They found the idea of schools for children of migrant labour to be an interference and a nuisance. With persistent efforts, however, cooperation started slowly. Factories allotted space, and designated a labour officer to coordinate with Janarth. Gradually, the support increased. Factories started providing water, some medical help, residence for teachers, space for the school and playground, etc. By the third year, factory managements provided 60 per cent of the school sheds, and 95 per cent schools had been given space for a small playground. Senior officials of some of the factories now attend school functions and take pride in the children's performance. In the coming years Janarth plans to push the agenda by ensuring that factory managements commit to abolishing child labour at work sites, and making direct investments in the education of the children.

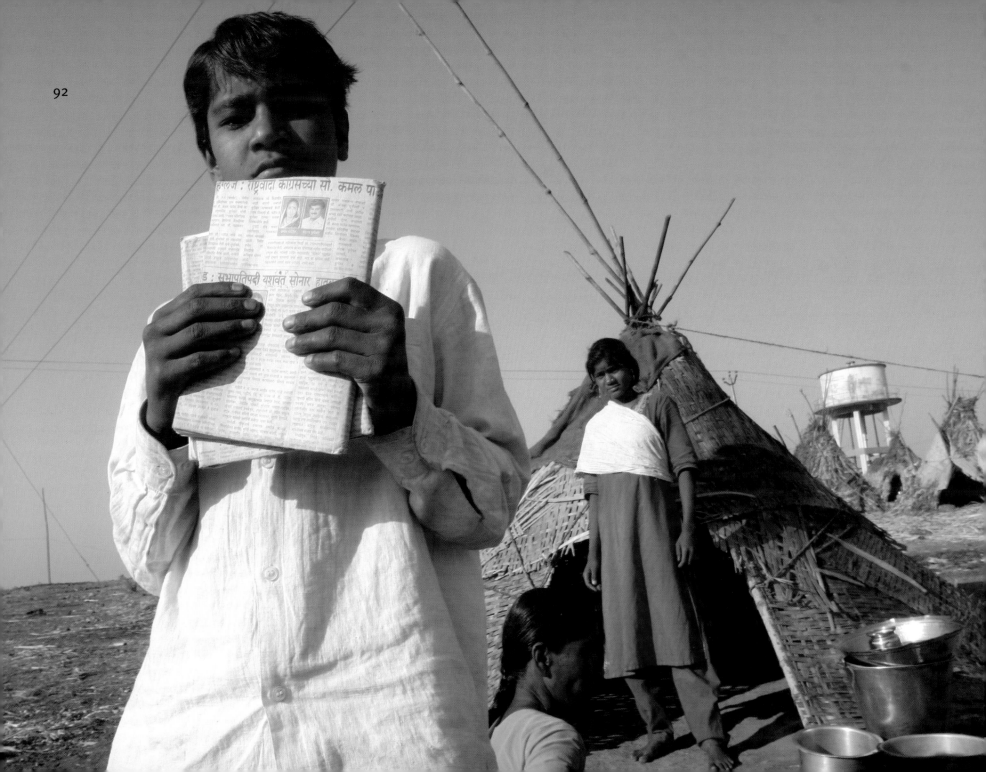

The advocacy agenda is to focus attention on the plight of migrant children and ensure their coverage under SSA.

ADVOCACY WITH THE COMMUNITY

The biggest advocacy 'tool' are the children themselves, who are now visible. Many hundreds of children — girls and boys — who were earlier cutting cane hidden away in the fields, now come to school every morning neatly dressed, and study and play cheerfully. The smaller ones who faced the most neglect now come to the pre-primary centres and are well looked after. School premises and classrooms are well organized. The youthful teachers and support staff exert themselves under the most trying circumstances in running these schools. They have built a strong rapport with the migrant community. Women make up 25 per cent of the teaching staff.

Parents meanwhile are making adjustments in their work so their children, especially the older ones, can go to school. Many mothers have expressed great satisfaction in being able to leave their girls in the safe premises of the schools. When parents are back from work, as one teacher said, "they keep an eye on the school". Another observation from a supervisor was, "They may not say or know much, but the school is important for them. If

We met a woman once at a work site of a sugar factory, where she had shifted a few days before from another factory that had closed operations early that season. She looked quite distraught, as she had lost many days of wages due to the unexpected halt in her work, the trouble of finding this new site, and then moving here with her family. There were no adult males with her, only two children, one a baby, and the other one a grown up girl. She had yet to erect her kopi, and her few belongings were lying about in the open. But she confidently informed us that she had put her girl already in the sakharshala nearby.

something is going wrong, they come and ask." They take pride in the physical training, games and other activities of the children. In the sakharshalas of one factory, parents' committees were formed at the initiative of the community and the staff. Now, this initiative is being promoted in all sakharshalas. Back in the village, many migrant families have started asking their mukadams (agents) to take them to factories with sakharshalas. Some mukadams have apparently begun to take this demand seriously, as they do not want to lose their labourers to other mukadams.

In the villages it has been encouraging to observe that non-migrant families, of a higher socio-economic status, are providing support to the hostels housing children of migrant parents. The hostel energizing the school and making the whole effort inclusive rather than exclusive is an important dynamic that should be capitalized on in the future. The increased demand for hostels from migrant parents in these and surrounding villages is another indicator of the positive community response. These are small beginnings, but they show the desire of the parents to educate their children, and their willingness to make all possible adjustments if proper opportunities are available.

ADVOCACY WITH GOVERNMENT

The advocacy agenda with the government is to focus attention on the plight of migrant children, and to ensure their effective coverage under SSA. This advocacy started to take shape once the programme was upscaled. AIF has been engaging in interactions with SSA at the central and state levels, while Janarth has worked at the state and local levels. The state government has accepted this model, in principle, as viable for the entire state.

It has also recognized Janarth as a competent technical resource for this work. However, implementation is a long way ahead. There were some initial successes — after three years of continous effort the government agreed to provide midday meals (MDM Scheme) in sakharshalas.

Efforts were also made to access funds for Janarth's programme under SSA.[48] After two years Janarth was able to access only 10 per cent of its total expenditure under SSA. This figure went up to 30 per cent in its third year. By the fourth year the state government decided to run seasonal hostels in all sending areas of the state for sugarcane and other migrations, accepting the SSA provision of Rs 6,800 per child per annum.

Janarth has been advocating the education of migrant children at the political level also by having questions raised in the legislative council. In 2005 the State Education Minister declared it mandatory for sugar factories in the state to have sahkarshalas. There have also been efforts at getting the sakharshala message into the media through radio jingles and press coverage. The organization has also been undertaking research and documentation on different aspects of sugar migrations, and is equipped with substantial data and information on this issue. It has also been interacting with academics and development agencies to raise awareness on the issue.

FUTURE DIRECTIONS

Programme coverage at work sites has already reached 12,000 children in 35 factories over seven districts. This is a critical mass. As mentioned earlier, now the attempt is to replicate this in a number of factories at this level, and intensify coverage of

children working for these factories. This entails reaching the mobile migrants or 'doki centres' more effectively. In the sending areas, Janarth plans to expand its work to about 25 villages covering at least two high migration pockets, and to achieve complete coverage of these with seasonal hostels and bridge courses. It also wants to strengthen government schools in these regions. Improved learning will be the focus at, both, factory sites and villages.

According to Janarth, the advocacy focus is to transit from external to SSA funding, and get the government to upscale this model to cover more sending and receiving areas. This will ensure elementary schooling for all migrant children. Janarth also hopes to develop into a technical support organization to the government and other agencies working on education of migrant children. Janarth's research is aimed at a deeper understanding of migration, and also looking specifically at migration into Gujarat and Karnataka in order to comprehend the larger picture of the sugar belt.

In Maharashtra AIF is trying to build a consortium of local NGOs to expand work on education as well as to address other critical aspects of migration such as alternative livelihoods, health and rights and entitlements. It is also working to initiate work in Surat and Belgaum through local NGOs, so as to reach the whole sugar belt. This should eventually lead to a dialogue between the governments of Maharashtra, Gujarat and Karnataka towards a joint plan for migrant children under SSA. The possibilities of initiating work in other sectors in Maharashtra, especially stone quarrying and brick making, are also being explored.

48. According to the EGS and AIE scheme under SSA the provisions for non-residential schools for migrant children are Rs 3000/- per child per annum, and for residential facilities Rs 6800 per child per annum.

The presence of the hostel in the village has given a boost to the local government school.

| THE SETU EXPERIENCE |

Gujarat is the hub of different types of migration flows. Setu works in Jamnagar and Rajkot in Saurashtra, which are coastal districts prone to earthquakes and cyclones. They are also regions of low rainfall and endemic drought. Along with Kutch, Jamnagar is officially designated an arid zone by the government. More significantly, the entire region is affected by salinity ingress, which is aggravated by depleting ground water and rising sea levels. Consequently the physical environment is degrading, and migrations for long parts of the year are on the rise.

Families from this region go in large numbers into salt pans, brick kilns, roof tile factories and charcoal making. Children accompany parents and drop out of schools. Migrants go to different work sites every year, and are also found to change sectors every few years depending on the climatic or market scenario. For instance, if excessive rains destroy salt pans, many salt workers shift to brick kilns, and so on. This unpredictability makes it difficult to keep track of families and children at the receiving end. Further, certain types of sites like salt pans and charcoal making are not amenable to schooling interventions. Conditions at these sites are extremely harsh for the adults, according to Setu, and even more so, expectedly, for the children. The number of children at one site is too small to make a school viable. The only sustainable solution for childcare and education is to prevent the migration of children to such sites, retaining them in the village in seasonal hostels.

COVERAGE

Setu began work in early 2004 in Jodiya, one of its migration prone

coastal blocks. The initial project plan envisaged coverage of 12 high migration villages in the first year, and expansion to cover all 50 villages of the block over three years. The idea was to scale up intervention to an entire administrative unit, and create a full fledged demonstration project for advocacy. However, the one-year engagement revealed the obvious — that migration defies administrative boundaries. It was intense in the coastal belt along the Gulf of Kutch cutting across two districts — Jamnagar and Rajkot — in the adjoining blocks Maliya and Morvi. There was less migration in villages further inland in Jodiya; therefore the earlier plan of covering a whole block was altered to cover the 50-60 villages in the migration belt of Jodiya, Morvi and Maliya blocks.

Conditions in Setu field areas are so harsh that the only solution is to prevent migration of children through hostels.

Setu enlisted the support of sarpanches of all project villages and turned community opinion in favour of this intervention.

49. Baseline study available with Setu and AIF.
50. Muslims 15 per cent; dalits 12 per cent and OBCs 76 per cent - all of which are 1.5 times the state average.
51. 40 per cent have completed primary education and 15 per cent high school.
52. Supply of water is a big struggle though.

In the first year Setu began work in 12 villages. The baseline study[49] revealed the migration rate in these villages to be 25 per cent, i.e. one in every four families went out in search of work. It is worth noting that the baseline year was a good rainfall year; in the previous year, which was a drought year, the rate was 35 per cent. Scheduled Castes, OBCs and Muslims form an overwhelming majority[50] amongst migrants. Of the 750 migrant families in the surveyed villages, only 11 (3 per cent) were from the upper castes. Education levels are low,[51] and the educated belong predominantly to the upper castes. The village with the lowest literacy levels also had the highest migration.

SEASONAL HOSTELS FOR MIGRANT CHILDREN

According to the baseline study, there were a total of about 3200 children of 6-14 years in the 12 project villages, of which 40 per cent were out-of-school, and 30 per cent dropouts due to migration. Setu interacted with the community for several weeks before starting the project work. They wanted to ensure the community, both migrant and non-migrant, wanted this intervention for their villages and would be a part of it. The initial response from migrants was of apprehension, and from non-migrants (who are generally of a higher socio-economic background) that of indifference. Setu enlisted the support of sarpanches of all these villages, and gradually turned community opinion in favour of this intervention.

In its first year Setu ran seasonal hostels in 11 villages to retain 174 children. No migration took place from the twelfth village because it had good rainfall and people managed to find work locally. Being their first attempt at running hostels, they chose to

start with boys in the first year, and cover girls from the second year onwards. In one village, however, about 20 girls were retained as an experiment in the first year. Proper facilities for girls were created in the second year and they were 25 per cent of the total number of children. Ninety per cent of the hostel coordinators today are women. Field staff, too, consists of 90 per cent women. Most of the staff is from the SC and OBC categories. It is commendable that today there is acceptance of the women hostel coordinators among the community as well as the schoolteachers, and they also have a say in community meetings.

The entire planning of the hostels was done with the involvement of the community. The hostels are run in community halls and clusters of empty homes of migrants. Each hostel has 20 children, one caretaker and one cook. Daily routines have been set for the children, which include morning exercise, tidying up the premises and rooms, study sessions morning and evening, and cultural activities. During the day all children go to the local government school. Many activities in the daily routine were a novelty for children initially, for example the brushing of teeth. The regular hot, nutritious meal is perhaps the biggest benefit for the children, followed by the developing of hygienic habits.[52] Setu introspected a great deal with respect to many things — for example whether to give children milk or not, or whether or not to provide fans in the hostel. The dilemma was between providing them the basic necessities, yet not alienating them from their life at home.

Contributions were raised in cash and kind from different quarters. The local people provided support when children fell sick, or in other unforeseen situations like when a child went

missing for a while. For Setu this was the first experience of its kind, and they went about it with great caution, aware of the tremendous responsibility of taking care of so many children without their parents. In the second year Setu established links with a local hospital and doctors. An effort was also made to raise community contributions, especially from migrant parents.

Evening classes at the hostels with study, games, singing and other activities are open to other local (non-migrant) children also. Several adults also collect and watch over the children, cheering them as they play and sing. This has garnered support from the non-migrant community. Nearly 400 non-migrant children have benefited from the evening classes. Migrant families working a short distance away, often come back to check on their children. Some migrants who had taken their children along in the first year, brought them back and left them in the hostels after seeing how they functioned. The demand for hostels has been multiplying every year.

In 2005-06 the overall work in Gujarat expanded to Kutchh and Saurashtra, and two more NGOs, Cohesion Trust and Yusuf Mehrally Centre (YMC) became partners. Coverage upscaled to 25 seasonal hostels and 450 children. Setu's own expansion remained limited to 12 hostels. While they had planned to double this number, due to reasons such as low migration and delay in tying up external funding they were not able to increase their operations. But the number of children increased to 215, and more importantly, hostel facilities were created for girls. The unpredictability of migration and its consequent disturbance in plans and budgets, however, remains and an estimation process needs to be streamlined.

IMPROVING GOVERNMENT SCHOOLS

Through this programme Setu reached out to many non-migrant out-of-school children in these 12 villages. They started by making an assessment of the government schools in the villages and listed their strengths and shortfalls. Subsequently, a rapport was built with the teachers and local bureaucracy. They joined in the admission festivals or praveshotsavs sponsored by the government at the start of the academic session and ensured the admission of all 6-year old children in class One. Over two years they have enrolled 416 children in government schools, of which 40 per cent are girls. Through their engagement with the government they were able to fill all of the 16 teacher vacancies that had existed in these schools for long. Setu is also trying to improve the delivery of the mid-day meal, and library books have been provided to all schools. Efforts such as these have helped win the support of teachers and local officials for this programme. In sum, after two years of engagement the government schools are functioning with far greater regularity, the pupil-teacher ratios, enrolment and attendance levels have improved, the stakeholder participation has increased with Parent Teacher Associations (PTAs) having become functional, and a strong link has been established between the hostel and the school.

SITE SCHOOLS AND BRIDGE COURSES

While Setu's work is centred in villages, they have felt the need, even if only as a temporary measure, to reach children who migrate to the work sites too. The purpose is to prevent child labour and gradually encourage all children to go to school. As a pilot project they ran some learning centres at brick kilns in the second year of the project. They plan to expand these to more work sites, including roof tile factories, and run pre-primary centres at all these places to cover the especially vulnerable 3-5 year olds. Interventions at salt pans and charcoal sites were found to be unworkable. Migrant children not covered at work sites will be put through bridge courses in villages at the end of the season.[53]

OTHER EFFORTS FOR THE MIGRANT POPULATION

Setu believes that efforts must be made towards mitigation of distress migration. During community interactions they found that many families lack even their basic entitlement papers. Many marginalized families were not in possession of birth and caste certificates, ration cards, land pattas and voter cards, which added to their vulnerability. As expected, the proportion was found to be higher amongst migrants. According to the baseline:

> 50 per cent migrants did not have PDS / BPL cards
> 40-50 per cent did not have birth certificates
> 90 per cent did not have caste certificates
> 10 per cent did not have voter cards

One of the programme objectives therefore was to ensure these papers for all families, specially the migrants. Setu has ensured that birth and caste certificates and land pattas have been issued to all people in project villages, and a BPL survey is being conducted in the villages.

ADVOCACY WITH THE GOVERNMENT

Setu is interacting with the SSA at the state level to push the agenda for migrant children. Press coverage of Setu's seasonal hostel programme in a national daily helped gain the attention

Over two years Setu has enrolled several hundred non-migrant children in government schools, of which 40 per cent are girls

53. Entitlement papers issues - ration cards 288, voter cards 473, birth certificates 275, death certificates, 68, land pattas 333 acres.

of the Gujarat government and others and Setu was asked to formulate a scheme for seasonal hostels for SSA. on the basis of which the government plans to start more hostels and site schools in the coming year. Setu has also been asked to help in identifying effective NGOs in migration prone areas of the state for taking on this work, as well as to provide them with technical support. The state government wants to map migration in the state, and is planning to do this in association with Setu.

The organization has been invited on several occasions to share their experiences in their work with migrant children at SSA meetings at the central level and in states such as Bihar, Andhra Pradesh and Madhya Pradesh, and also at meetings and workshops organized by other agencies such as ILO, etc.

FUTURE DIRECTIONS

Setu plans to expand the programme until it reaches full coverage of the 50-60 villages in the migration prone belt of the Gulf of Kutchh. The Paul Hamlyn Foundation has also started funding the replication of this work in one block from the second year. The state government has sought Setu's help in starting 50 hostels and site schools for migrant children in the sugar, salt and fisheries sectors in Kutchh, Saurashtra and South Gujarat. Setu will now shift focus to improving learning outcomes with special focus on migrant children.

After bringing the Kutchh based Cohesion Trust (marine salt-pans) and YMC (fisherfolk) on board, AIF is planning to further enlarge the consortium. Setu will be in the lead role. This consortium is expected to raise a stronger voice of advocacy for the education of migrant children in Gujarat.

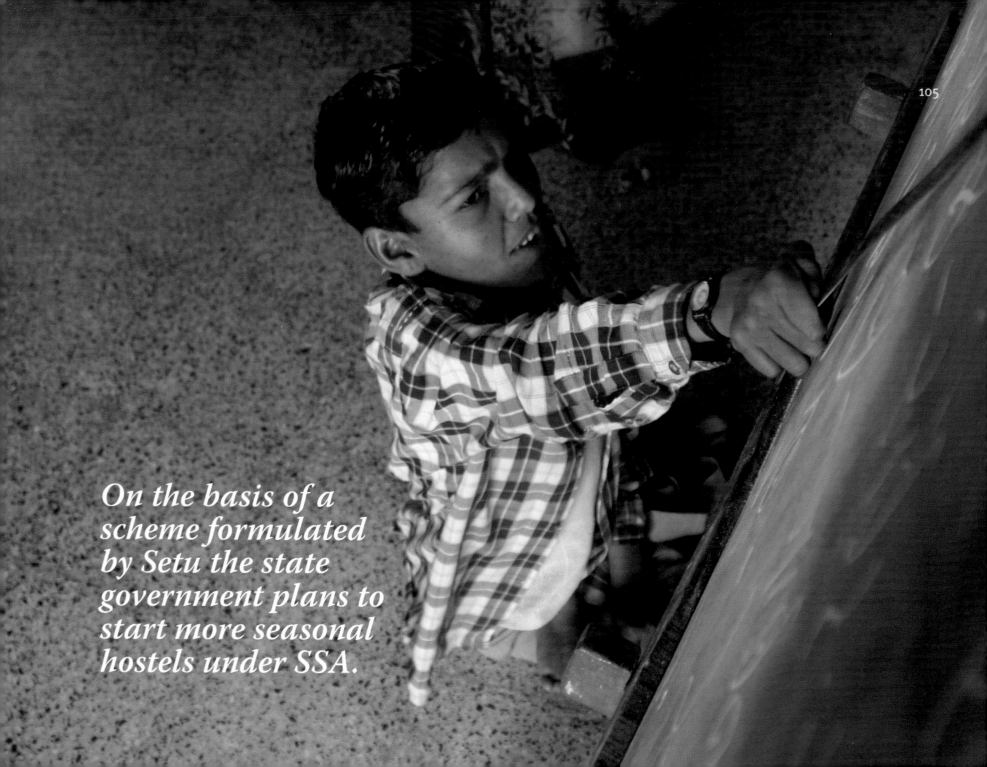

On the basis of a scheme formulated by Setu the state government plans to start more seasonal hostels under SSA.

| THE VIKALPA AND LOK DRISHTI EXPERIENCE |

Migrations from western Orissa to the brick kilns of Andhra Pradesh are perhaps the most distressful of all, as indicated by field evidence and some photo and film documentation. In district Bolangir, where this migration is the most intense, five of its nine blocks are greatly affected. Bolangir alone sends out 100,000-150,000 migrants each year, and the trend is rising with time, as more and more villages and habitations come into the fold. The migration period is for eight to nine months — starting post Dusshera and ending with the monsoon the following year.

Seasonal labour migration has its roots in the drought years of the mid 60s. The first migrations were to Bhilai and Raipur, expanding to Bombay, Calcutta, UP etc. These migrations were largely of males only — families stayed behind in the village — and accumulative in nature. A small percentage turned into permanent migration. The eighties however gave way to a far more insidious process of organized and blatant exploitation of cheap labour. The demand came from brick kilns in Andhra Pradesh, resulting in huge migrations of impoverished tribal and dalit families. This also expanded to the textile industry of Surat (Gujarat) and the construction sector in various regions. But today about 70 per cent of the total migration from this district is to the brick kilns of Hyderabad.

Over the last two decades the kiln owners have spread a sophisticated network of agents and sub-agents to numerous villages in districts of western Orissa, penetrating remote poverty-afflicted areas. The hub of local activity is Kantabhanji, a small town in Bolangir. It is from here that the coordination takes place between the Telugu contractors and kiln owners in

Hyderabad on the one hand, and the Oriya sub agents who recruit people from the villages, on the other. During a certain period in October, Kantabhanji is found to be teeming with Telugu speaking people — every lodge is full, as contractors or sardars camp here to organize their labour. Large-scale cash transactions take place between contractors of Andhra Pradesh and Orissa, for advances to migrants as well as for bribes. Nova khai, the local harvest festival in September is the time when agents secure labour by advancing small sums of money (Rs 6,000-12,000) per unit for a man, woman and child. The other children of the family also accompany the parents. By November

Hostels are run in government schools, community halls and space offered in people's homes

Many children in these hostels got a full meal and a blanket for the first time in their lives.

large streams of people leave their villages and board trains packed with labour, all going to Kantabhanji to be transported to brick kilns in Andhra.

THE SEASONAL HOSTEL PROGRAMME

Vikalpa in Bolangir district and Lok Drishti in adjoining Nuapada district have worked in the area of livelihoods for long, but both are relatively new to education. Their livelihoods work has mitigated distress migration in their project areas, but neither had previously worked on migration issues directly. In November 2004 they began interventions for education of migrant children in eight villages each. The intervention comprised running seasonal hostels to retain migrant children, and improving the functioning of local government schools.

The first task was to break the entrenched practice of 'work units', which necessarily included a child. Parents were at first apprehensive that agents would not take them without the child, but many got convinced and stood up to agents to refuse to give their children. Simultaneously, the NGOs talked to the agents and where necessary even pressurised them on legal grounds to keep children out of work units. Many agents agreed but there were also reports that several others decided to bypass these project villages, and recruit their labour from elsewhere.

About 400 migrant children stayed back in 16 hostels to continue with their schooling. Many of the hostels in Orissa were set up in government schools, a significant point to note. Others ran in community halls and space offered in local peoples' homes. Each hostel had 30 children, a coordinator and a 'mother'. The coordinator managed the hostel, and made links with the school and the community. The mother cooked for and took care of the children. Mothers were selected from among the destitute women in the village. They made a great difference to the atmosphere of the hostels in the way they cared for these children whose parents were so far away. They would lovingly oil and plait the girls' hair, feed the younger children, tell stories, stay up all night if a child was sick, and so on. Not surprisingly, the children developed great bonds with the mothers. Sometimes parents made long distance calls to check on their children. The support of self-help groups was also enlisted, and many took over the cooking responsibilities for the hostels. Many non-migrant children attended the supplementary classes that were run in the hostels, morning and evening, regularly. About 250 children who had migrated that season were covered on their return in educational bridge courses during summer months.

Many children in these hostels got a full meal and a blanket for the first time in their lives. Proper food and cleanliness transformed them and when they returned, many parents could not recognize them! Over two years, parents have started to notice the change in the children's performance, conduct and health.

In 2005-06 the work was upscaled to cover about 1900 migrant children in 65 villages in three of the five high-migration blocks of Bolangir, and two of Nuapada. While in the first year, hostels were run mainly for boys, and very few girls could be included, in the second year, 40 per cent of the children in hostel were girls, and separate living arrangements were made for them. In cases where there was a shortage of space in the hostel, people in the village offered space in their homes for girls to come and sleep every night along with the mother. This was

achieved due to sustained efforts of the women SHG members to encourage girls to stay back and study. This also indicates the trust that parents have in the local NGOs. In addition to Vikalpa and Lok Drishti, two more NGOs of Bolangir — Adhikar and Jan Mukti Anushthan — have been brought on board. Vikalpa is providing technical support to them.

IMPROVING GOVERNMENT SCHOOLS

"Schools in these areas are nothing much to talk about," according to Vikalpa and Lok Drishti, "and children in grade IV and V cannot spell properly or do simple arithmetic." The NGOs attempted

The first task for the NGOs was to break the entrenched practice of 'work units', which necessarily included a child.

NGOs are building awareness among stakeholders... on the consequences of a child being forced to leave school and go to the brick kilns.

111

CASE STUDY 3CASE STUDY 3

to strengthen the VEC through regular community contact. This helped improve enrolment and the attendance of both teachers as well as students in the schools. The hostel coordinator supported the government teachers, and encouraged them to visit the homes of children. The midday meal scheme also improved. In some villages, the community undertook small repairs in school buildings with their own contributions. In other places community members made an assessment of the existing infrastructure of the school, like the tubewell, toilets, condition of class rooms, teaching materials and so on, and presented a memorandum to the panchayat, block and district officials on what was required. The NGOs are trying to build awareness among all stakeholders including the community, local officials and PRIs on the magnitude of the problem of migration, and consequences of a child being forced to leave school and go to the brick kiln.

An important part of the intervention in Orissa is initiating registers in villages in which details of migrant families are recorded by the community (information on family members who migrate, name of mukadam, advance amount, destination, time of leaving, etc). This is the first step towards documenting these workers, about whom so far there have no records have been maintained. This availability of information about the migrants with the community will help reduce their undue exploitation at work sites, and enable people in the villages to be in touch with them. Such records maintained over a few years will help to understand migration patterns better. These registers are maintained by the palli sabha, the local village body. Vikalpa and Lok Drishti feel that the creation of a database on migration by involving the panchayat will help in making the

government acknowledge the scale of migration. Forums have also emerged in some villages for returning migrants to share their experiences, and this makes the community aware of the reality of work sites. Vikalpa and other partners have made a joint visit to the Hyderabad brick kilns to see the situation first hand at work sites. They are also using media to highlight the plight of migrant children.

MOBILE TEACHERS AND
BRIDGE COURSES IN ANDHRA PRADESH

In 2004-05, ActionAid ran work site centres in three districts of

54. About 200 workers including 88 children were released from bondage from a brick kiln in Rangareddy district
55. Rs 3000 per child per annum, which is less than half of what is required to run a residential facility

Andhra Pradesh — Rangareddy, Medak and Nalgonda — covering about 1500 children who migrated from Orissa. ActionAid negotiated with the government schools located in the vicinity of the brick kilns to allow space for classes for these children. Mobile teachers from Orissa were appointed to teach them.

ActionAid ran health camps at brick kilns, through which over 700 infants were immunized, 250 pregnant women got health check ups, and 3000 children, women and men were able to get general health check ups. ActionAid is providing legal aid to the workers against exploitation, releasing workers, including children, from bondage,[54] and ensuring compensation for the rescued workers. Efforts are also being made to provide temporary membership to migrant workers with local trade unions.

ADVOCACY WITH STATE GOVERNMENTS
Orissa

Sarva Shiksha Abhiyaan, Orissa, has a programme for seasonal hostels, but the provisions under it were very low in 2004[55] (subsequently they have increased), and implementation was weak. The arrangement was that Vikalpa and Lok Drishti would access the government provisions (Rs 3000 per child per season), and additional funds (Rs 4000 per child per season) would be provided by AIF. The objective was that these hostels with adequate funds and facilities would serve to demonstrate how such a programme could be run effectively. This would raise demand from the community for better provisioning and implementation of the government programme.

The coordination with SSA at local and state levels was taxing for the two NGOs. The fund flow — from the state through district and block offices to the panchayat — met with obstacles and delays. Frequent transfers of officials at state and district levels compounded these problems. Dialogue continued with SSA at central and state levels, but despite positive responses from the upper levels, ultimately, only a part of the funds was received by the two NGOs, and that too at the end of the migration season. This compromised the quality of programmes.

During 2005 SSA revised its provisions for residential programmes from Rs 3000 to Rs 6800 per child per annum. Therefore the external fund was seen as a bridge fund to the NGOs to tide over the delays. Continuous engagement has led to an improved rapport between NGOs and SSA officials and the fund flow from the government has improved.

ANDHRA PRADESH AND ORISSA

With the efforts of ActionAid annual meetings are held between the Andhra and Orissa governments to initiate policy change for migrant workers. Rural Development, Labour, Education and Women and Child Welfare departments of the two states have participated, in addition to NGOs and development agencies, to discuss a range of issues like:

> Documentation of migrant workers, in the sending and receiving areas;
> Transfer of their entitlements, like PDS grains, to their destination points;
> Dialogue with employers; steps to ensure minimum wages and basic facilities
> Improvements in children's schooling at brick kilns

FUTURE DIRECTIONS

In the years to come, the plan is to enlarge the consortium, and encourage more local NGOs to work with migration issues, not only with respect to education, but also alternate livelihoods, rights and entitlements. In the very backward and migration-prone districts like Bolangir, the provision of 100 days of work every year under the National Rural Employment Guarantee Act (NREGA) will also go a long way towards mitigating distress migration. Vikalpa, Lok Drishti and other partners are planning to work towards effective implementation of this Act in collaboration with other agencies. Proper capacity building on NREGA is also to be done by the four NGOs.

Efforts from NGOs have helped improve attendence of both teachers and students in schools.

114

| ROLE PLAYED BY AIF |

It is important to highlight here the role played by AIF, the funding agency, in helping build this significant programme for education of children of seasonal migrants, covering different sectors and geographies. AIF started by identifying the major sectors that attract migrant labour and the areas where this is happening on scale. Since there were no NGOs working on education or migration within these geographies, AIF decided to engage with the existing livelihoods and other NGOs and gradually built their capacities in these areas. The prerequisites they looked for in their prospective partners were strong community linkages and an empowerment based approach.

AIF has helped its partners design their programmes within their contexts. Since the experience base in this area is limited, the programmes have been of an evolving nature. For instance, the initial programmes began at one end of migration — either sending or receiving — but soon the need to work at the other end was realized. Also, the programmes were not allowed to remain at a small level. Emphasis was, and is, placed on upscaling each year, thus dealing with the dynamics of expansion. The idea was to reach a critical mass (in some cases in terms of number of children/sites/villages, in others complete or representative coverage of a high-migration belt or pocket), which would help advocacy with the government. Expansion is undertaken strategically after mapping and surveys. Each year new dimensions have been added to the programmes (enlarging of age group, pedagogic inputs, livelihoods and rights-based inputs, etc). A great deal of cross learning has taken place between different partners, through field visits and joint reflection, periodically. Gradually, a model of intervention has emerged, which is being further tested and refined in newer projects.

Another critical perspective that AIF has provided to its partners is that of UEE. All programmes are geared towards UEE in their field areas, which implies that while the intervention has a migration-focus, it goes on to include all children — migrant as well as non-migrant. Thus in every village all out-of-school children are being reached, and the local schools are being revitalized to deliver for all children.

Emphasis on engaging with the government is another element added by AIF. All partners are now effectively involving the government at local and state levels. They share experiences and strategies at the central level too. Being in line with the SSA objectives and framework these projects have a greater potential to demonstrate and inform the government how to address the difficult category of migrant children in different states. Advocacy for change in provisioning and systems is also being pursued where necessary.

The problems that have arisen in these projects have also been similar. For instance:

> Since these interventions are only for part of the year, staff cannot be employed for the whole year. In villages the hostel coordinators can still be employed for all 12 months, and during non-migration months run bridge courses and support government schools. But in the case of site schools this is not possible. Janarth has struggled with the inefficiency of turnover, fresh recruitments and retraining of sakharshala teachers. Now it tries to recruit more teachers from sending areas and re-employ them in the villages. But a perfect solution is still to be found.

> Migration is unpredictable. If the rains are good and less people migrate, the capacity created in the project can go waste; if there is drought and more people go, more hostel space might be needed. All NGOs have faced these situations. Also, circumstances such as a strike by the sugarcane union in Maharashtra, the substitution of regular bricks by hollow bricks in Gujarat (for Narmada dam construction), a cyclone causing a shutdown at salt works and people shifting sectors, have thrown project plans out of gear.

> The timing of families leaving villages, and returning can never be known for sure. This has implications for examinations and bridge courses.

These are being dealt with at project level through refinement of systems. But they do have policy implications.

Overall the capacities of partners have increased. Going forward, AIF is helping raise more local NGOs in each area to engage on these issues, with old partners playing a lead role. The idea is to build local capacities to deal with migration, expand coverage, and improve advocacy. The number of partners in the three states has grown to eight. AIF is also exploring possibilities of working in other significant migration sectors and geographies such as stone quarrying, construction, agriculture, etc. There are also other types of migrations like the child-only migrations, short duration repetitive migrations, and round the year migrations which have their own challenges. Coordinated work among different types of agencies will be needed to address migration comprehensively and holistically.

All programmes are geared towards UEE in their field areas, which implies that while the intervention has a migration-focus, it goes on to include all children — migrant as well as non-migrant.

LEARNINGS FROM INTERVENTIONS

| PROGRAMME ASPECTS |

INTERVENTIONS with seasonal migrants involve taking into account the larger migration reality, as well as the specifics of the particular sector and geography being addressed. Moreover, experience shows that the intervention needs to be comprehensive, encompassing the places of origin of migrants as well as work sites, for it to be effective and sustainable. This usually involves working across several districts and often across more than one state.

While innovative solutions have been found for many difficult categories of children, the factor that differentiates children of distress seasonal migrants from other out-of-school children is their mobility. Planning for children whose families are not settled, but on the move, warrants fundamental rethinking of approaches and models to ensure universal access, retention and quality (UEE). Some key elements of programme design, culled out of the experiences of the four NGOs are shared below:

WORKING AT SENDING AND RECEIVING ENDS

The challenge in migration is of mobility, with families spending part of the year in the villages and part at work sites. Educational interventions for children of seasonal migrants thus need to cover both the sending and the receiving ends. Multiple options must be put in place to maximize coverage-in villages and at work sites (seasonal hostels, site schools, bridge courses, etc.)

In the long run, however, the village needs to be seen as the base for the main interventions and the worksite for the supplementary ones, for the following reasons:

> The quality of schooling at work sites is bound to be limited
> The shift every year between site school and village school is difficult for a child to make, and leads to drop outs.
> Children living at work sites cannot escape the hardships there, which seriously impact their development.
> As the migrant family has no control over where it goes from year to year, there is no guarantee the child will find a work site school each year (unless all sites have schools).
> No interventions are possible at shifting work sites in case of short duration agricultural migrations.

In villages it is possible to invest in proper facilities for children to stay while their parents migrate. In this way they can go to the government school without disruption or discontinuity, and complete their elementary and high school. Work sites, on the other hand, cannot be equipped for this. Monitoring of universal coverage can also happen effectively only in villages, not at work sites.

ADDRESSING SCALE, SPREAD AND NATURE OF MIGRATION

Both sending and receiving areas have a large scatter — several contiguous villages/blocks/districts may be affected by out-migration, similarly in-migration (work sites) is also generally spread over large areas. The distance of migration is the other issue to be reckoned with: Migrations may be short distance (intra district, inter district), as well as long distance (intra state, inter state). Thus, for interventions to be effective they must have a large coverage. The dynamics of migration renders small-scale programmes ineffective. And for long distance migrations,

The challenge in migration is of mobility, with families spending part of the year in the villages and part at work sites.

or interstate migrations it may be necessary to work collaboratively with more than one agency.

Another factor that needs to factored in is the duration and timing of migration. Some migrations take place once in a year for a long duration (6-8 months), while others are for shorter durations several times a year; still others have no clear seasonality. The strategy of intervention in long duration migrations will be different from that in short duration migrations. For instance, the former may have seasonal hostels while the latter may have flexible, round the year stay facilities.

The case studies indicate that all interventions started as pilot projects but upscaled each year, moving towards a critical mass of geographical coverage and coverage of children. Some have attempted to reach full coverage of a high migration belt or pocket, for example Janarth in Maharashtra started with coverage of 600 children in one district but reached 12,000 children in 8 districts in 3 years. The programmes in Gujarat and Orissa also grew twice and four times respectively in one year. This was achieved through upscaling by individual partners as well as getting more NGOs on board. It also strengthened advocacy with government.

THE CHALLENGE OF PLANNING AND MANAGEMENT

Education programmes have to work within two annual overlapping cycles — the migration cycle and the school academic cycle. Moreover, different interventions come up at different points of time (hostels and site schools in November; bridge courses in May) and in different places (villages, work sites), which is a challenge in terms of planning and logistics. The planning has to centre on the timing of the movement of these populations. Different migrations begin at different points of time

Education programmes have to work within two overlapping cycles — the migration cycle and the school academic cycle

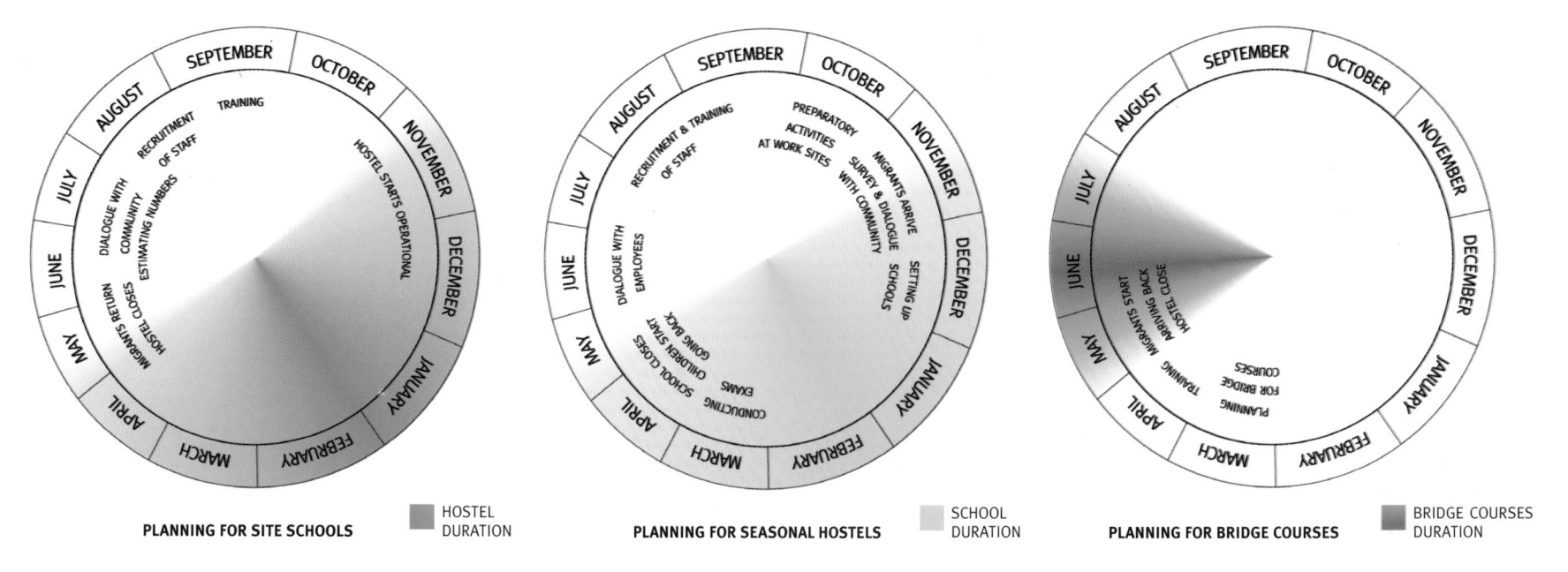

PLANNING FOR SITE SCHOOLS ■ HOSTEL DURATION

PLANNING FOR SEASONAL HOSTELS ■ SCHOOL DURATION

PLANNING FOR BRIDGE COURSES ■ BRIDGE COURSES DURATION

and are for varying durations. The sugarcane, brick and salt migrations begin around November and end around May. Thus hostels in villages need to be in place before families start to leave. Similarly site schools need to be ready by the time they arrive at work sites, and bridge courses, when they are back from migration. Any delay at any stage will throw the process out of gear. There has to be a detailed preparatory process prior to each intervention, which includes recruiting and training of staff, identifying space for school/hostel, survey of migrant families, mobilization of parents and communities, and in case of work site interventions contacting employers, and so on. This also involves managing work in different locations — sending and receiving areas — and if two agencies are working collaboratively, mutual coordination.

DEALING WITH UNPREDICTABILITY

The unpredictability of seasonal migrations determined by climatic and market conditions, poses a major planning challenge. First, the fluctuations in the number of migrant families — the initial estimates of how many people will migrate may differ significantly from how many actually do. This has implications for the capacities created for hostels and work site schools. Secondly, variation in the length of the season from year to year — if the season is shortened, the work site school planned for six months may close after four months, if the season extends hostels may have to run for longer. Plans for annual examinations and bridge courses may go awry. The challenge is to continuously refine the estimates on the one hand, basing them on several data sources (community, mukadams, employers, rainfall, crop productivity,

The unpredictability of seasonal migrations poses a major planning challenge.

*In the long run the village n
interventions, and work sit*

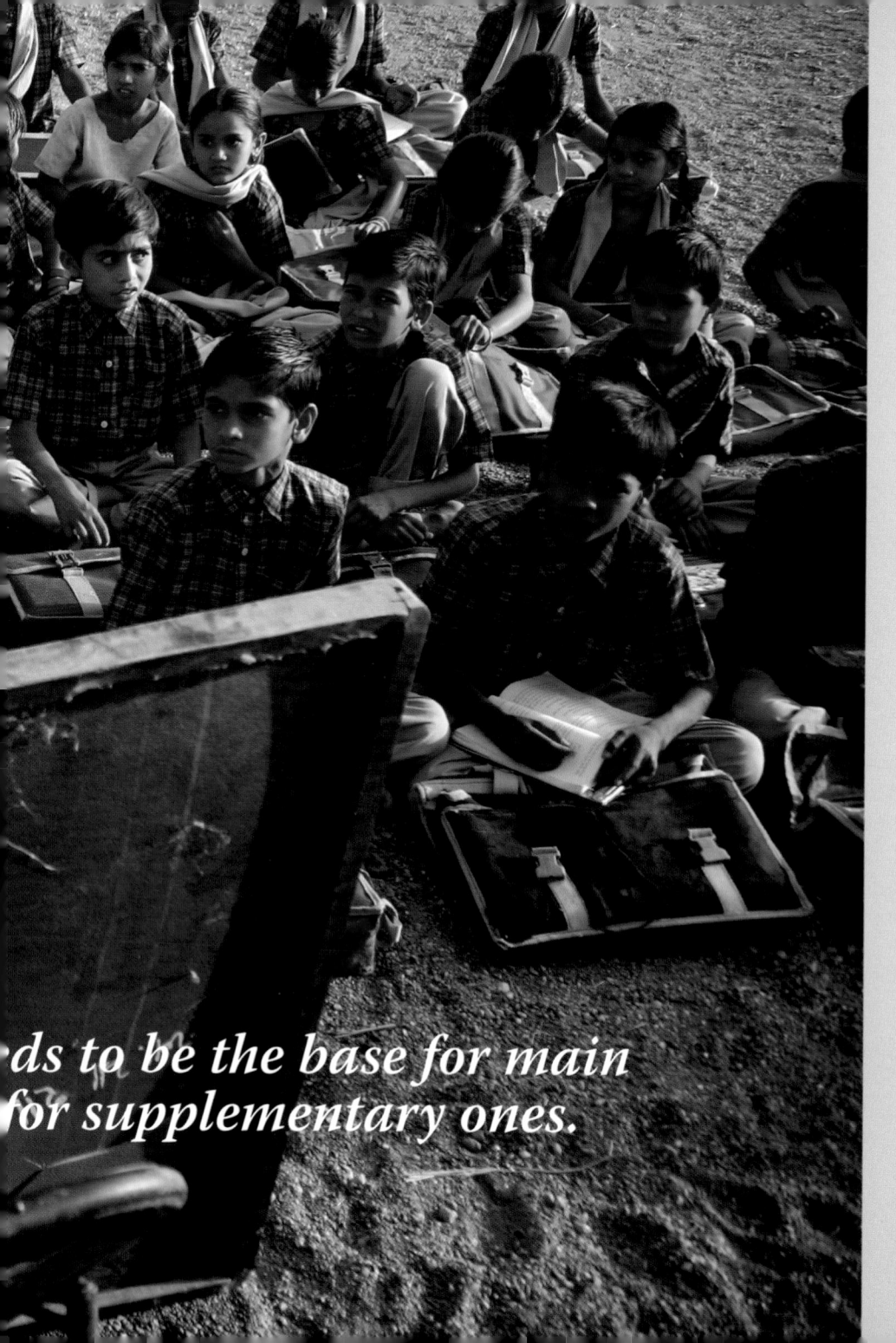

ds to be the base for main for supplementary ones.

123

related government decisions, market trends, etc), and on the other to have flexible plans and alternate courses of action to accommodate sudden, unforeseen changes.

ENGAGING WITH COMMUNITIES ON THE MOVE

Working with mobile communities is a different ballgame from working with those that are settled. Migrant communities spend part of the year in villages and part at work sites. Work sites have a sort of stability of population as different families are brought there each year. Some sites may have just a handful of families (salt pans, charcoal). Moreover, the labour force at these sites is highly controlled. They remain under strict surveillance of contractors, often in almost captive conditions. Any attempt by outside agencies to interact with them is not received well by employers, and they are likely to increase their harassment. NGOs, like Janarth, who have major interventions at work sites, have so far maintained a tactical silence on issues regarding adult labourers, remaining focused on children's education in order to just be allowed to run schools there. Although at sugarcane sites, parents are beginning to take interest in schools, and committees are being formed but the various limiting factors above do raise the question whether a larger mobilization at work sites is even possible, and around what issues.

The time spent in the villages by migrant communities is too short, and goes into putting their homes together again, meeting their many neglected household needs and struggling to make ends meet. Before long they are preparing to leave again. The already existing distance between these and other socio-economically better-off communities in the villages is increased due to the long absence of migrants each year. Their participa-

*Working with
mobile communities
is a different
ballgame from
working with those
that are settled.*

THE EMERGING MODEL

The model emerging from the experience of the four NGOs for comprehensive coverage of migrant children involves interventions simultaneously in sending and receiving areas, and multiple options of schooling spanning both villages and work sites. The mainstay of the model is the local government school, and all alternative measures lead the child back to the government school. The four dimensions of the model are as follows:

Seasonal hostels in villages: Given the hazardous nature of work sites, and the lack of any facilities of proper care and education there, it is imperative that parents have the option of leaving their school-age children behind in the villages. The model envisages setting up seasonal hostels in villages that run through the migration period, enabling children to stay back in the village and attend the local school. While separating children from their parents is not desirable, given the unacceptable levels of distress at work sites, this is an option that many migrant families have wanted! Parents who can make their own arrangements to keep their children in villages have already been doing so. In project areas of NGOs, the demand for hostels has been rising every year.

Schools/centres at worksites: For children who do not stay back in a seasonal hostel and continue to migrate with their parents, the model envisages the provision of work site schools/centres. The objective is to prevent child labour, ensure that children are in adult care in a safe and clean environment, and have opportunity to learn and play. The nature of the school/centre, however, will depend on the nature of the work site. At the relatively better organized work sites, like sugarcane 'tyre centres', with proper space and physical facilities and adequate number of children available, a more formalised school set up is possible. On sites like brick kilns where settlements are smaller and the physical facilities rudimentary, at best, activity centres can be run. SSA provides for a centre even for five children. The third category of work sites where mobile migrants work and keep shifting location

every few weeks, e.g. charcoal making, sugarcane doki centres, etc schooling interventions are difficult. Short duration agricultural migrations that take place several times a year cannot be addressed through site schools. Thus the emerging thought is that more and more children should eventually start opting for the seasonal hostel in the village. But the choice should finally lie with the parents.

Bridge courses in villages: For children who do not stay back in a hostel, and migrate to a work site where they do not find a school, the model provides the option of a bridge course in the village on their return during the monsoon months. This would link them back to the local government school.

Bridge courses and work site schools/centres are more in the nature of transient measures, and seasonal hostels are the longer term solution for migration prone geographies. While initially all three options need to run simultaneously to ensure every child gets covered somewhere or the other, and falling through the cracks is minimized, but over time the need for bridge courses and site schools should reduce, and more and more children should have the option of staying back in hostels and going to the village school.

Strengthening local government schools: An important dimension of the model is to address the local school itself. Inadequacies in school functioning, like teacher shortage, text book shortage, non accountability, low performance, lack of supervision, and over and above low learning levels lead to drop outs, not only of migrants but also other children. Unless the school itself is improved, efforts to retain migrant children would yield no results. Thus strengthening of local schools and ensuring coverage and retention of all children migrant and non-migrant is an essential part of the scheme. Improvement in classroom pedagogy in order to improve learning levels, and building greater sensitivity among teachers and officials towards migrant children are also critical. This needs to be done through mobilizing the community, and effective engagement with teachers and block and district officials.

tion in social and governance forums, due to the nature of their livelihood pursuit, gets reduced to minimal levels. Even their interactions with each other become limited. How this might impact on the social scenario is a subject to be researched. But mobilization of migrant communities is indeed a challenge. Stock methods do not work. And clearly unless this aspect of their marginalization is addressed, their voice will increasingly become smaller. This has to be seen with a fresh perspective. Case studies, however, point to the potential there is in education bringing together migrant and non-migrant communities.

BUILDING NGO CAPACITY

The NGOs in migration-prone geographies generally work on livelihoods. Very few address migration directly. And even fewer are focused on education. If this work has to spread then building the interest and capacities of more NGOs on these issues is what is needed. This is possible to do, as seen in the case studies, with extensive ground level engagement by NGOs in villages and work sites, to understand the dynamics of migration in their respective areas. Side by side, they would have to engage with children, schools, classroom pedagogy, and with the education system at all levels.

ENLARGING THE RESEARCH AND INFORMATION BASE

There is much that needs to be understood about migration, therefore research and documentation ought to be an essential part of all work on distress seasonal migration. For instance, the detailed baselines prepared by some of the NGOs studied above have helped in understanding the picture of migration in their areas. As coverage expands, and data becomes available over wider areas,

its extrapolation will also help in arriving at estimates of migration over larger geographies. Qualitative studies on different aspects of migrations also need to be undertaken to arrive at a comprehensive understanding of given sectors and geographies.

| POLICY ASPECTS |

It is imperative that planners and policy makers address the issue of distress seasonal migration holistically — the departments of education, labour, rural development and other relevant institutions must study the specific circumstances of this labour force to restore to them their due as citizens of the coun-

There is much that needs to be understood about migration therefore research is essential.

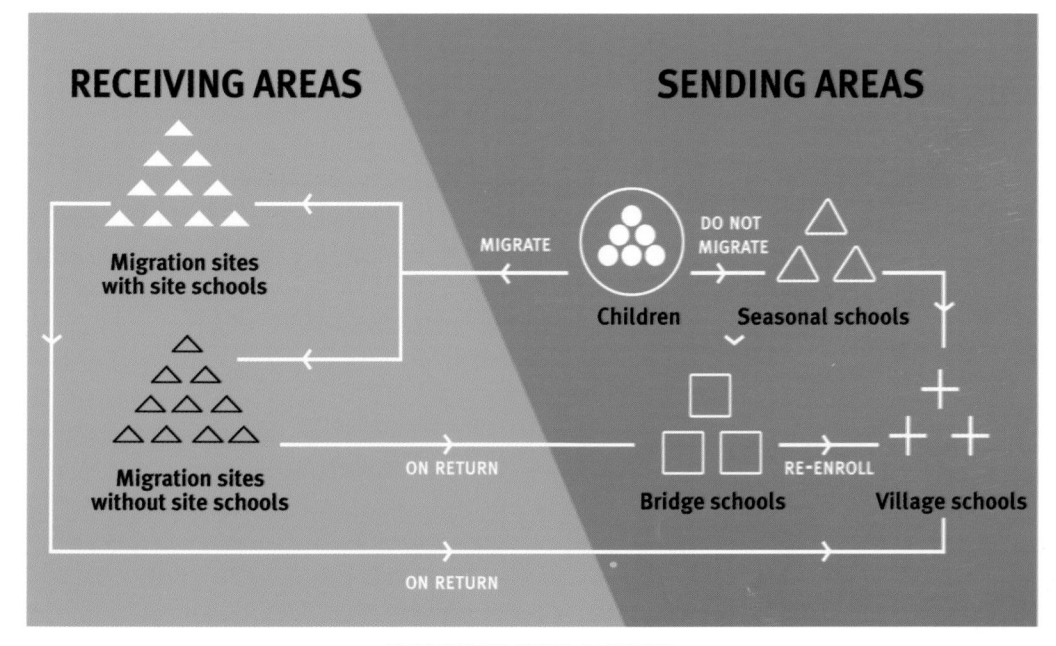

THE EMERGING MODEL: A DIAGRAM

try. Discussed below are policy implications for ensuring UEE for children of migrant families under SSA. Also highlighted are the areas that need to be looked at with respect to rights and entitlements, health, information and alternative livelihoods.

1. ROLE OF THE GOVERNMENT WITH RESPECT TO EDUCATION

While there have been some attempts to plan for migrant children under the District Primary Education Programme (DPEP), the forerunner of SSA, these were not comprehensive or sustainable. To work towards UEE, children of seasonal migrants need to be seen as a special focus group, and annual work plans of each state must reflect data and time bound plans for their coverage. Some keys areas for policy intervention are:

> **The larger issue of out-of-school children**

– There is a debate on the number of out-of-school children in the country today. The Ministry of Human Resources Development (MHRD) figures of about 10 million in 2003-04 (down from 35 million in 2001-02) are under question.[56] The estimated number of children out of school due to seasonal migration is about 6 million, and this is just one of the numerous categories of out-of-school children. This has serious implications for the education scenario. An immediate fallout is the conflict between surveys of out-of-school children by NGOs in their areas and the government figures. This obstructs the work of NGOs and their access to SSA funds. In the context of migrant children, two questions need to be asked:

– Have the state surveys ensured the coverage of families that migrate seasonally? Most surveys are done in the months of December and January, when migrant children are away at work sites.

– How is the term 'out-of-school' to be seen in the context of migrant children, many of whom are enrolled but remain out of school for several months every year?

> **Assessing seasonal migration in states**

Data gaps lead to policy gaps. To effectively address the issue there is a need to understand seasonal migration in each state in terms of its type, pattern, scale and spread. Broadly this would entail studying and evaluating:

– *Geographies:* Sending areas, i.e., agriculturally distressed districts and blocks that send out labour, need to be identified. Similarly, receiving areas where work sites are located, need to be mapped. Since migration defies artificial boundaries specific migration prone pockets or belts would need to be marked out.

– *Sectors:* The different sectors attracting families, especially child labour, have to be identified. For each sector, the work site areas need to be demarcated.

– *Migration flows:* Labour flow may be intra block, inter block, inter district and inter state. Often a given area may both send and receive labour. Migration flows need to be mapped.

– *Magnitude of migration:* Work site surveys during migration months and village surveys during non-migration months will give the magnitude of adult and child migrants.

Data on these parameters will help generate a picture of migration in each state, which could then serve as a base for planning and policy change.

> **Joint planning between districts and states**

While migration implies mobility between districts, educational planning, like all other planning, is focused on a district as a fixed entity. Once migrant children leave their home district they

56. This decrease implies that the last two years have registered whopping increases of 12 million and 13 million in enrolment respectively. But considering that in the preceding 12 years the increase in enrolment has been only around 1-2 million every year, this increase in the range of 20 million - over the last two years - warrants careful examination. Ref: Elementary Education in the Tenth Plan - Promise, Performance and Prospects (2005), Govinda and Biswal.

While there have been some attempts to plan for migrant children in the past, these were not comprehensive or sustainable.

SSA needs to have a system of joint planning between sending and receiving districts/states.

become external to it; they are not counted in the work district either. SSA needs to respond to this, by having a system of joint planning between the sending and receiving districts. The planning would have to take into account labour that circulates among various sending and receiving districts, and interstate migration. It is essential to develop mechanisms that address all such scenarios.

> **Making schools responsible**

Government schools have so far failed to respond to the drop out due to seasonal migration. This neglect is visible at cluster, block, district and upper levels. For this scenario to change, schools as well as the system have to take on the responsibility of migrant children's education in terms of access, retention, learning and completion of the elementary cycle. Some systemic issues that need to be revisited in this regard are:

– Rules and procedures related to readmission, attendance,

examination and promotion to be modified to suit the needs of migrant children.

– Schools to track migrant children through child identity cards, tracking registers, etc.

– Learning support to be provided for children when they return from migration through bridge courses, remedial classes, etc.

– Local administration to monitor coverage, retention and learning of migrant children.

The long-term strategy however must be to prevent migration of children by establishing seasonal hostels in villages. This would ensure their participation in the mainstream school and completion of their school education.

> **Provisions and fund transfer issues**

The EGS and AIE scheme for out-of-school children under SSA is fairly proactive, and takes note of migrant children as a category. It also encourages states to take the support of NGOs to cover difficult categories. An important element of this scheme is making financial provisions on a per child basis (instead of the former system of per school basis), thus reflecting a commitment for every child. Yet its implementation is falling short of expectations. Many states show reluctance to engage with NGOs and part with SSA funds. Also they continue to look at fund disbursement in the earlier mode instead of looking at 'per child' costs. The problem gets further compounded at district levels. This disconnect between centre, state and district is a barrier for NGOs and for the proper implementation of the EGS & AIE scheme.

While the government provisions[57] for various types of alternate schooling facilities are not unreasonable, field experience suggests that there is a case for revision of these limits. The NGOs in this study are running their interventions in areas with harsh natural conditions or very low levels of development. Many basic needs of these hostels and schools cannot be met at the present levels of provision,[58] and are being externally funded. But the sustainable solution is for the state to increase its own provisions.

> **Advocacy with employers**

The government must ensure that child labour at work sites, under the garb of piece rates and work contracts, stops and employers are penalised heavily. As per the Child Labour Act, they should abolish child labour at their work sites, and instead provide for the education of the children of the migrant labourers in their employ.

2. OTHER ASPECTS OF MIGRATION AND THE GOVERNMENT'S ROLE

The life of migrant families is precarious, and the odds against them are numerous. While education is important to prevent the next generation from getting sucked into the distress migration cycle, for these efforts to sustain, other critical aspects of the migrants' situation need to be simultaneously addressed, such as labour rights, entitlements, health, information needs and alternative livelihoods. It is not possible for any single agency to do all this and therefore collaborations are necessary. Some aspects to be addressed are:

> **Rights and entitlements**

– Enforcement of labour laws and regulation of work sites to ensure proper working and living conditions

– Transfer of entitlements such as usage of PDS / BPL cards at work sites

– Running of special buses or trains during migration period to facilitate the massive labour movement (specially for the

The government must ensure that child labour at work sites, under the garb of piece rates and work contracts, stops and employers are penalised heavily.

57. Rs 3000 per child per annum for non residential and Rs 6800 per child per annum for residential programmes

58. For example temporary structures for sakharshalas, tankers for drinking water in Kutchh, lighting at night in hostels in Nuapada and Bolangir where villages are not electrified, etc.

brick kiln migrations from Orissa to Andhra Pradesh)
- Empowering migrants through accurate and timely information
- Providing temporary membership for migrant labour of labour unions in destination areas
- Inclusion of 'seasonal migrants' as a category in the census
- Measures to ensure migrant labourers can exercise their franchise at work sites if elections take place during migration period.
- Revision of Interstate Migrant Workmen Act (1979) and creation of legislation for intrastate migration

> **Health**
- Making health and medical facilities available at work sites, specially for women and children
- Coverage of children in immunization drives at work sites
- Provision of protective gear to labourers (helmets, boots, gloves, ear plugs, etc)
- Provision of insurance cover to labourers, and ensuring of timely compensation claim when needed
- Investment in technological upgrading of tools and implements to reduce physical stress

> **Alternate livelihoods**

The long-term solution for distress seasonal migration is to create livelihood options in villages. This would help eliminate the 'distress' element from migration, and if people will migrate, it will be by choice, on terms favourable to them, and their children's education will not be affected. The livelihoods programmes of many NGOs have helped mitigate distress migrations. Some significant examples are the successful watershed work by Samaj Pragati Sahyog (SPS) in Dewas district of MP and the work done by Aga Khan Rural Support Program (AKRSP) in

The long-term solution for distress seasonal migration is to create livelihood options in villages.

Gujarat, which appear to have stemmed the trend of distress migration over the last decade. Interactions with the community in SPS field areas indicate that families that regularly migrated for agricultural work to farms of large landowners have, for the last few years, enough agricultural output and local work to sustain them. Now employers come knocking on their doors, and if they acquiesce, they do so on their own terms, demanding 3-4 times higher payment rates than before, and choosing the time of their convenience. Moreover, children who migrated earlier are now going to school.

> **National Rural Employment Guarantee Act (NREGA)**

The National Rural Employment Guarantee Act (NREGA), which ensures 100 days of employment to the rural poor in selected backward districts, has immense potential to mitigate distress seasonal migration. If 100 days of work is made available in the post monsoon months in migration prone villages, it will significantly reduce distress migration. The experience of Sankalp and Mamoni in district Baran of Rajasthan clearly demonstrates this. Their effective implementation of the Right to Food Scheme (the forerunner of NREGA) amongst the very backward Sahariya tribes in their field areas brought down distress migration by 30 to 40 per cent in a large number of villages. The role of local NGOs will be crucial in controlling this scheme, ensuring that work is made available at the appropriate time i.e., in the post monsoon months. This is the critical period for the migrant community, when their need for work is the greatest, and in the absence of employment they succumb to the advance offered by contractors. This should also result in productive assets being created for village, which will reduce distress migration in the long run.

CONCLUSION

The UNDP Human Development Report, 2005 says

> Human development is about freedom. It is about building human capabilities — the range of things that people can do, and what they can be. Individual freedoms and rights matter a great deal, but people are restricted in what they can do with that freedom if they are poor, ill, illiterate discriminated against, threatened by violent conflict or denied a political voice. That is why the 'larger freedom'[59] proclaimed in the UN Charter is at the heart of human development.

It goes on to add, "The most basic capabilities for human development are leading a long and healthy life, being educated and having adequate resources for a decent standard of living. Other capabilities include social and political participation in society."

It needs to be seen how the above vision can be practically achieved for some of those living in the most difficult circumstances. Although large sections of the impoverished families in India live with limited freedom, populations who have become uprooted from their homes and are forced to be on the move in search of livelihoods for the most part of the year present a case for inequity amongst unequals. They fare worse in every respect mentioned above as compared to those of similar socio-economic status who can afford to be in their villages all the year round.

At their work places, far removed from home district or state, deprivation and exploitation is again of a higher order than were they doing similar work in their villages. The invisibility of the operations of sectors dependent on migrant labour, and the disempowered status of these nomadic families appear to have given license to the employer to flout all possible work norms and ethics. To break the cycle, the children must be provided proper care, exposure and education so that they have alternate opportunities.

Migration for livelihoods cuts across social classes and categories. Migration is generally seen as an opportunity for asset building, exposure and personal growth. Moreover it is regarded as a matter of individual choice. All this, however, presupposes at the very least a 'level playing field' in economic terms, and a state apparatus that protects the rights and entitlements of its citizens wherever they may go. But when the field is tilted, and the apparatus, functioning smoothly for the privileged, becomes defunct for the underprivileged, and 'choice' is replaced by 'compulsion', it becomes an issue of wider concern. Today it is a reality that tens of millions of impoverished rural families who migrate seasonally remain uncovered by the state welfare and legal net. Distress migration creates long-term indebtedness and perpetuates below subsistence livelihoods. It denies labourers any possibilities of upskilling or upward mobility. Even after 25-30 years families have continued to migrate at the lowest paid unskilled levels.

The question is not whether seasonal migration is desirable or not but, rather, how can the distress element be eliminated, and people's dignity and choice restored to them?

No major state today is untouched by the phenomenon of distress seasonal migration. The developed states have a greater responsibility in terms of addressing the in-flows, and

59. The vision of 'larger freedom' in the Human Charter holds out the promise of a new pattern of global integration built on the foundations of greater equity, social justice and respect for human rights.

Today it is a reality that tens of millions of impoverished rural families who migrate seasonally remain uncovered by the state welfare and legal net.

those less developed have the challenge of addressing outflows. Further, every state needs to understand and address the complicated and ever-changing circulation of migrant labour that goes on within its boundaries. This is by all evidence a growing phenomenon with more agriculturally distressed regions coming into its fold. The number of affected villages is on the rise, and within them the number of families resorting to seasonal migration is increasing. Whereas earlier the landless and land-poor used to migrate now, with greater incidence of crop failure, the band is broadening and even those with more land are joining the stream.

Employers in different labour intensive sectors are systematically exploiting peoples' distress. Labour recruiting networks of contractors and subcontractors operate with remarkable efficiency. They make sure they leave no negotiating space for migrants whatsoever. Even if labourers in one area try to organize and demand higher wages, they are bypassed, and recruitments are made from elsewhere, leading to depressed wages and increased control. Over time and at a macro level this has translated into widespread displacement of local labour with migrant labour. Facilitated by the much improved transportation infrastructure, these networks now span vast areas, and are penetrating the remotest pockets, especially tribal pockets.

Employers access family labour at rock bottom prices,

entrenching people in a cycle of dependency to ensure their availability year after year. The system of work contracts, cash advances and piece rate payments form the economic basis for this entrenchment and are designed with great ingenuity in favour of the employers. Through work contracts they escape all responsibility to the labour force producing the work. Cash advances create debt bondage, which ensures continuity of labour supply year after year. Piece rates help get away from minimum wage regulations, and also draw children into work although they are not 'employed' as such. Such rampant exploitation and disregard of all labour and child rights, however, can thrive only in an environment where the state is unconcerned and the mainstream society unaware.

Child labour is a given part of family labour and, needless to say, is almost unpaid. It would have to be seen to be believed how children from the youngest ages get apprenticed into adult work at migration sites, and become full-fledged labourers by the time they are 11 or 12 years of age. To make matters worse, child labour — from being casual — is being institutionalized with greater segmentation of processes and specific sets of operations being delineated for children. Some labour contractors now bring only children, and there are sectors that access only child labour. Entrenching child labour ensures this phenomena continues generation after generation.

Another matter that warrants the most urgent focus from all quarters is the situation of female migrants. It is difficult to comprehend in how many ways the hardships and exploitation faced by women and girls are intensified as they are forced to leave the security of their homes and villages. They face this all through the travel and the months of stay at the work sites.

There is also considerable differentiation within the broader category of 'distress seasonal migrants'. Even in the impoverished strata, those of higher caste, and having some assets and resources at their disposal are able to secure work on better terms (more organized sectors, higher advances, settled work sites) as compared with others who do not (lower advances, shifting work sites, changing sectors, etc). Differentiation also happens on account of caste, religion and region — for example the higher ranked sectors and within them, better paid work is dominated by OBCs, while lower ranked sectors and less paid work runs on dalits. There are also trends of certain sectors accessing labour from certain regions and pockets — tribal areas are specially targeted by some sectors. Age, skill and physical strength also play a role. Men above 40 years, women, those with some disability or poorer health conditions, work at increasingly compromised levels (until they are weeded out). The conditions on the ground are multifarious and messy, and need to be painstakingly unravelled before any effective programmatic and policy interventions can be made.

Another dimension of these migrations is that while technology has transformed the outer world beyond recognition, the work sites look the same as they did half a century ago. There is no impact of technology on the drudgery of processes at these sites; workers still employ the same heavy and unwieldy tools and implements as the older generations did, with no design inputs. Since protective gear has never been a feature of these work sites, there is no question of its upgrading!

The industries involved have failed to own up to their responsibilities towards migrant labour and their children, and have instead been tacitly benefiting from the highly underpaid adult labour and almost free child labour in the garb of 'work contracts' and 'piece

The challenge of dealing with seasonal migration is basically the challenge of dealing with mobility. The massive, multi-layered state apparatus spanning the country, however, is designed only for dealing with settled populations. Migration is traditionally seen as people leaving one location to settle in another. Seasonal migration, although prevalent in the past, used to take place on a limited scale. Therefore, all policy and planning was done with a focus on settled populations. The recent decades, however, have witnessed the escalation of this phenomenon both in magnitude and complexity, and according to all indicators will only increase in its scale and reach. The state apparatus has not only failed to keep pace with this changing scenario pushed by a rural livelihood collapse and consumerist urban boom, but it is as though it has even failed to take notice of it. The systemic response to migrant populations has to start with a fundamental re-examination of the policy and planning paradigm, and adjustment within it to accommodate altogether new requirements of this section of citizens.

The country is focusing on basic development issues towards achieving the Millennium Development Goals by 2015. The Sarva Shiksha Abhiyan, armed with sufficient flexibility, funds, and the will at the national level provides the vehicle to move towards UEE by 2010. This is the time for the education administration to take the bull by the horns and turn the situation around for migrant children, and migrant people.

rates'. To turn this around, they must be made to face their legal and ethical commitments which is a job to be proactively done by the government, supported by media and development agencies.

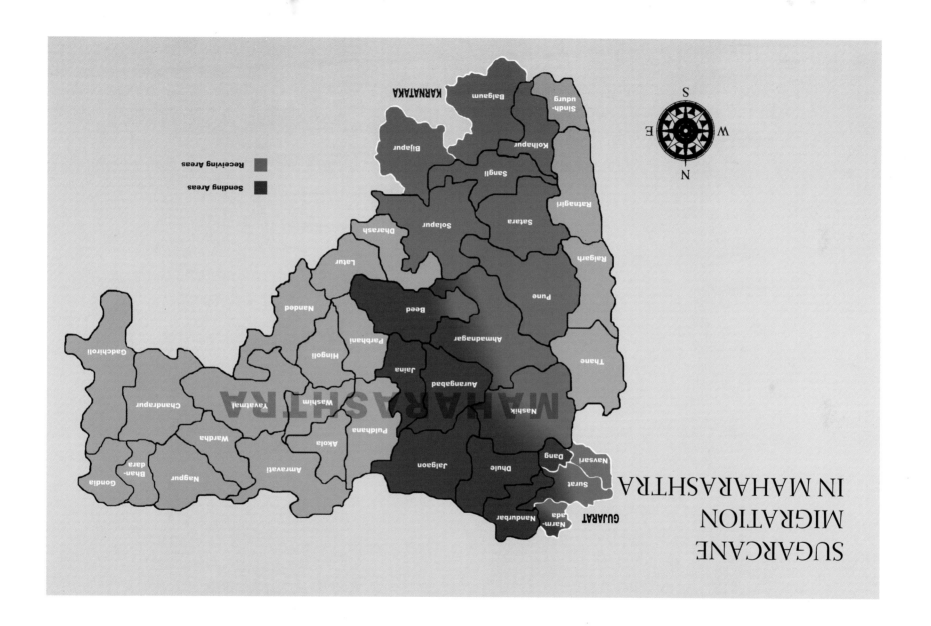

SUGARCANE
MIGRATION
IN MAHARASHTRA

Sending Areas
Receiving Areas

KARNATAKA
GUJARAT

MAHARASHTRA

Gondia
Bhan-dara
Nagpur
Gadchiroli
Chandrapur
Wardha
Amravati
Yavatmal
Akola
Washim
Buldhana
Nanded
Hingoli
Parbhani
Latur
Dharash
Jalna
Aurangabad
Beed
Nashik
Jalgaon
Dhule
Nandurbar
Narm-ada
Dang
Surat
Navsari
Ahmadnagar
Pune
Thane
Raigarh
Solapur
Satara
Sangli
Ratnagiri
Kolhapur
Bijapur
Belgaum
Sindh-udurg

MIGRATION
IN GUJARAT

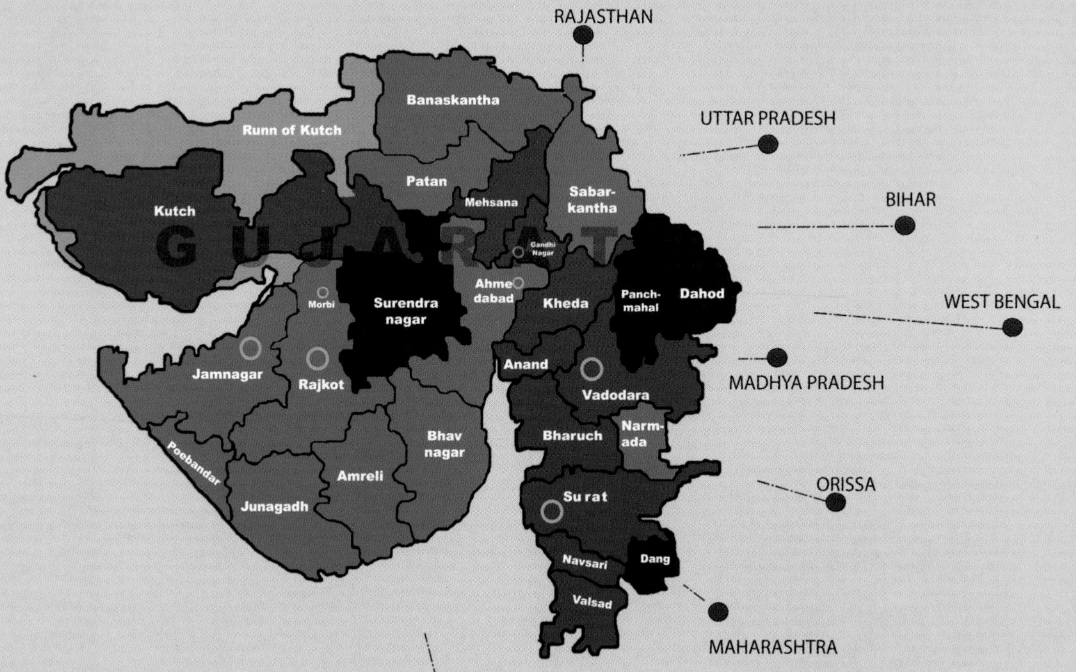

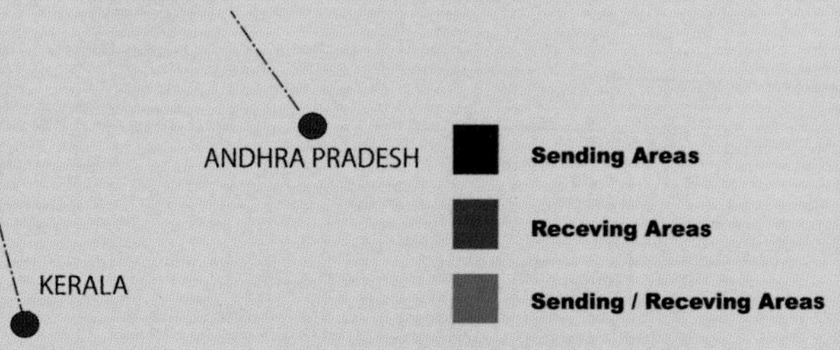

States	Type of Migrants/Workers
Rajasthan	Salt Pan, Power Loom,Roof Tiles, Ceramics
Uttar Pradesh	Power Loom , Brisk Kiln, Textiles
Madhya Pradesh	Construction, Brick Kiln, Roof Tiles
Orissa	Diamond, Salt Pan, Power Loom
Andhra Pradesh	Salt Pan, Diamond, Construction
Maharashtra	Sugarcane cutter, Power Loom
West Bengal	Jari Work, Goldsmith
Kerala	Fish Processing
Bihar	Power loom ,Textiles, Jari-Work

Sending Areas

Receiving Areas

Sending / Receiving Areas

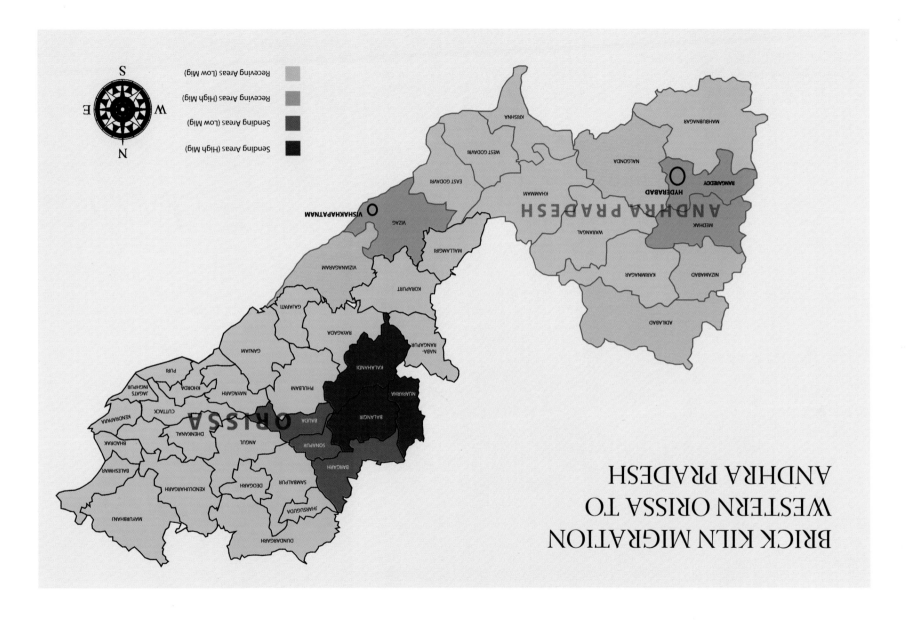

BRICK KILN MIGRATION
WESTERN ORISSA TO
ANDHRA PRADESH

Sending Areas (High Mig)
Sending Areas (Low Mig)
Receiving Areas (High Mig)
Receiving Areas (Low Mig)

SELECT BIBLIOGRAPHY

Action Aid 'From Hunger to Suffering... A Journey: Migrant Workers in the Brick Kilns — Interventions Report', Secunderabad

Breman, Jan and Arvind N. Das, (2000), *Down and Out: Labouring Under Global Capitalism*, Oxford University Press.

Breman, Jan, (1994), *Wage Hunters and Gatherers*, Oxford University Press.

Desai, Mrinalini, (2005), 'Janarth Sakharshala — The Sending Villages Report', National Centre for Advocacy Studies, Working Paper 23, Pune.

Deshingkar, Priya and Daniel Start (2003), 'Seasonal Migration for Livelihoods in India: Coping, Accumulation and Exclusion', Working Paper no. 220, Overseas Development Institute, London.

Ganguly, Varsha (1999), 'Living Conditions of Salt Workers in Kutchh', Setu, Ahemdabad.

Government of India (1979), 'Inter-state Migrant Workmen Act', 1979.

Government of India (2005) 'Right to Education Bill 2005', Draft.

Govinda, R., and K. Biswal, (2004): 'Elementary Education in 10th Plan: Promise, Performance & Prospects — A Background Paper for Mid-Term Assessment', NIEPA.

Katiyar, Sudhir Kumar (2005), 'Short-term Migration in South Rajasthan — Incidence and Impact', Draft Report, Sudrak, Udaipur.

Mosse, David, and Sanjeev Gupta (2005), 'On the Margins in the City: Adivasi Seasonal Labour Migration in Western India', *Economic and Political Weekly*, July 9, 2005.

National Commission for Enterprises in the Unorganised Sector (2006), 'Social Security for Unorganized Workers Report', New Delhi.

National Sample Survey Organization, Government of India (1999-2000), 'Migration in India 1999-2000' (2001) NSS 55th Round.

Rafique, Abdur and Ben Rogaly (2003), 'Internal Seasonal Migration, Livelihoods and Vulnerability in India: A Case Study', Paper for Regional Conference on Migration Development and Pro-poor Policy Choices in Asia.

Setu, 'An Overview of Migration in Gujarat' Ahmedabad.

Srivastava, Ravi and S.K. Sasikumar (2003), 'An Overview of Migration in India, its Impacts and Key Issues', Paper for Regional Conference on Migration, Development and Pro-Poor Policy Choices in Asia.

Srivastava, Ravi (2005), 'Bonded Labour in India: Its Incidence and Pattern', Special Action Programme to Combat forced

Labour, Declaration /WP/43/2005, International Labour Office.

UNDP (2005), *Human Development Report 2005 — International Cooperation at a Crossroads: Aid, Trade and Security in an Unequal World,* New York.

Venkateswarlu, Davuluri (2005), 'Unilever and Child Labour in Hybrid Cottonseed Production in Andhra Pradesh — Allegations & Response', Action Aid UK.

NOTE ON PHOTOGRAPHS
Setu, Gujarat
The photos in Gujarat were taken in Jodiya block of Jamnagar district in Setu's project villages. The village and hostel pictures were taken in villages Jhinjuda, Solankinagar, Kharachiya, Padabekar and Madhapar. Brick kilns were photographed in Amran and charcoal makers and their living spaces in Balambha forests. Salt pans were covered in Navlakhi. These were also photographed in Vira in Anjar block of Kutchh district. The fishing migrants were photographed on Luni Bandar in Mundra block of Kutchh district.

Janarth, Maharashtra
The photos taken in Maharashtra covered the sugarcane cutting sites and migrant settlements around Indapur Sugar Factory in district Pune and Kagal Sugar Factory in district Kolhapur where Janarth's sakharshalas operate. The seasonal hostels were photographed in Ashti block of Beed district, and villages covered were were Morala, Khadakwadi, Nagtala and Sanghavi. The migrants in trucks were photographed in and around village Kutarwadi. The picture of the rows of bullock carts were taken on the Ahmadnagar-Aurangabad road. Some of the small sugarcane settlements (doki centres) as well as cutting sites were also shot on this road as well as on subsidiary roads.

Vikalpa and Lok Drishti, Orissa
The seasonal hostels run by Lok Drishti were photographed in village Khamtari, in Khariyar block of Nuapada district. Those run by Vikalpa were photographed in village Sonmudi, in Khaprakhol block of Bolangir district. Pictures were also taken in village Dokra of Belpada block and village Babejuri of Muribahal block in Bolangir district. Programs here are run by NGOs Adhikar and Jan Mukti Anushthan respectively.

Hyderabad, Andhra Pradesh
Brick kilns were photographed in Bommalramaram Mandal in Nalgonda district, which borders the city of Hyderabad.

ACKNOWLEDGEMENTS

THIS BOOK is an outcome of the efforts of many people. First and foremost are those who have been tirelessly executing the programmes on the ground — Pravin Mahajan of Janarth, along with Gautam Landge, Arun Patil, Shalikram, Mrinalini Desai and Ms Murugkar; Ashok Srimali of Setu, together with Danabhai Gohil, Daud Saicha, Ashok Sawariya, Maldeo Bamrotia and Allarakha Sheikh; Dr S.K. Pattnaik of Vikalpa, with Sanjay Mishra and Sudhir Guru and Dr Abani Panigrahi of Lok Drishti, with Bhubneshwar Raut and Nabin Mishra. There are many other highly motivated individuals in these teams, whose contributions have been tremendous. It is primarily this work which has helped open up the area of distress seasonal migration in its varied aspects, and which forms the content of this book. A special thanks to Carolyn Stremlau and Ajit Chaudhary for being comrades in this work.

I am indebted to several people who have spent considerable time discussing issues of seasonal migration with me. I have been fortunate to travel with many of them in the field. I specially mention Umi Daniel, Vivek Pandit, Pravin Mahajan and Sukhdev Patel who shared with me their extensive knowledge of the brick, sugarcane and salt sectors. I also thank Motilal, Bastu Rege, Dharmendra, Kalyan Dangar, Rajesh Kapoor, Jatin Patra, Bhajaram Sahu and Sheeshram for helping me build my understanding with respect to a range of other sectors and geographies. The organizations visited were ActionAid, Hyderabad, Vidhayak Sansad and Santulan in Maharashtra, Ganatar, Yusuf Mehrally Centre and Cohesion Trust in Kutchh, Sankalp and Bodh Shiksha Samiti in Rajasthan, Samaj Pragati Sahyog in Dewas, and the work of SSA in Panna in Madhya Pradesh. I am really grateful to these organizations for their generosity with their time and resources. The interactions with people working in the field, migrant families, children, labour contractors, PRI representatives, teachers, local officials and others were the richest sources of insights on this subject.

My discussions with Prof Ravi Srivastava, Prof Jean Dreze, Prof Dipankar Gupta, Dr Ben Rogaly and Dr David Mosse enabled me to place the ground level understanding of seasonal migration in an academic framework. Discussions with Babu Matthew helped me get a grasp of the legal dimension of the issue. Here I must specially thank Bishnu Prasad Sharma, an advocate in Kantabhanji, who has been working intensively on the rights of brick kiln migrants in Orissa for the last many years. My very special thanks to Achyut Yagnik for spending many hours explaining and re-explaining the complexities and diversities of migration in Gujarat.

I thank Sumit Bose, Dr Poonam Batra, Shanti Jagannathan, Ajay Mehta and Dr Anita Dighe for their inputs in evolving this work. The contributions of Dr Govinda and Dayaram are specially significant in helping build a perspective on education both from the programme and policy points of view. I thank them for always taking out time to discuss this work, and adding to it.

We at AIF are grateful to Vrinda Sarup for taking interest in these programmes and paving the way for addressing migrant children in the larger UEE initiative under SSA. We also thank Meena Bhatt in Gujarat , M.S. Padhi in Orissa, K. Chandramouli in Hyderabad and Narendra Kawde in Maharashtra for doing the same in their states. And I have no way to thank Dhir Jhingran for 'never saying no' and for his constant support both in develop-

ing ideas and pushing this agenda forward.

Important inputs have been received on the manuscript from Dr R Govinda, Achyut Yagnik, Dayaram, Prof Ravi Srivastava, Shanti Jagannathathan, Dr Poonam Batra and Dr Mihir Shah. Suchitra Sheth has been my moral and 'technical' anchor while putting this book together. She has read the maximum number of drafts, given painstaking comments, helped me to appropriately structure the document, and prevented me from committing blunders. I also thank her for her creative inputs related to design and publishing. I am indebted to Urvashi Butalia for her editorial expertise, and for helping me bring out the gender dimension with greater clarity. I thank Uzma Mohsin for her excellent design inputs. My sincere gratitude to Namrata Asthana, Suman Nag and Tarun Sharma for their contribution in improving the presentation of the book.

The closest come the last — my colleagues in AIF. Shankar Venkateswaran is the single most critical person in shaping this work as well as the contents of this book. Lata Krishnan and Pradeep Kashyap are the two pillars of AIF in US and who have stood solidly behind this work, and made it happen. They continue to relentlessly build a constituency among donors for this most marginalized section of the population in India. I also thank Raju Sharma for his enthusiastic and energetic support.

Finally, my deepest gratitude to Prof Jan Breman who was kind enough to meet me on his visits to India to discuss the progress of this work, and for taking time to read the manuscript and provide detailed comments, which have helped to considerably improve it.